Additional Praise for Unleashing Your Inner Leader

"I clearly remember the moment… I announced a new promotion at SAS and Vickie announced the launch of her coaching business. That was when I became Vickie's first client. Vickie led me through many of the exercises that she details in this book—discovering my strengths and values, learning to delegate and ask 'what' questions, using my personal brand, and building my leadership legacy. Vickie tells you it won't always be easy. And yes, it took time for these concepts to become a natural part of my leadership style and to reap the rewards of choosing roles that I love; while delighting my team by 'treating them the way they want to be treated'. This book is a must read.

> —Kristin Rahn, Analytics Industry Executive (former SAP Vice President, SAS JMP Business Unit leader, AAA Analytics leader)

Unleashing Your Inner Leader is a standout in the plethora of "how to be a better leader" books. Coach Vickie shares her real life experiences coaching over 4,000 managers, directors and executives in becoming better leaders. The concepts and tools coupled with real life examples of success in this book provide an easy to follow roadmap that will make you a better leader."

> —Melissa Church, Vice President, Optum

"Clarity of communications in a cluttered world of competing messages is all-important. As a non-profit manager, you must know precisely the value you bring to the organization and the attributes your team contributes to communicating the message your organization seeks to impart to its constituency. This self-knowledge and organizational clarity takes analysis and refining. Coach Vickie offers a roadmap of how to get started and provides guideposts along the way to measure your progress. 'Know yourself and know your brand', she says. Hard to do, but she offers tools to support her good counsel."

> —Roy M. Henwood, CAE, Former Agribusiness Trade Association CEO and Government Relations Professional

Coach Vickie's approach is direct and simple. What's more important than uncovering your Inner Leader and using it to play your best game possible? Business professionals know where they want to go and this book shows them how to get there. The real-life examples and case studies in this resource are a must read.

> —Sandy Carter, General Manager, Ecosystem Development

This book reflects the wisdom of an experienced, practical leadership coach whom I continue to use in my leadership programs because of her effectiveness with a wide variety of clients. Vickie Bevenour has encapsulated the lessons of her work with thousands of leaders in the form crisp insights, compelling case examples, and effective action exercises that can be used to enhance your own leadership development trajectory. She is someone worth listening to.

> —Sim B Sitkin, Professor of Management and Founding Faculty Director of the Fuqua/Coach K Center on Leadership and Ethics at Duke University

WILEY & SAS BUSINESS SERIES

The Wiley & SAS Business Series presents books that help senior-level managers with their critical management decisions.

Titles in the Wiley & SAS Business Series include:

For more information on any of the above titles, please visit www.wiley.com.

Unleashing Your Inner Leader

An Executive Coach Tells All

Coach Vickie
Condolff Bevenour

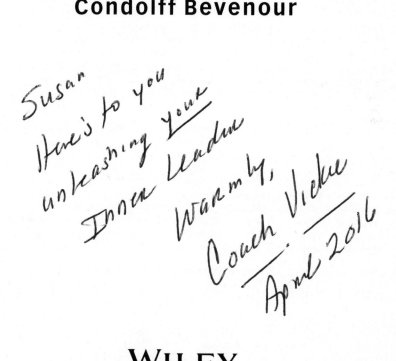

Susan
Here's to you
unleashing Your
Inner Leader

Warmly,
Coach Vickie
April 2016

WILEY

For general information on our other products and services or for technical support,
please contact our Customer Care Department within the United States at (800)
762-2974, outside the United States at (317) 572-3993 or fax (317) 572-4002.

Wiley publishes in a variety of print and electronic formats and by print-on-demand.
Some material included with standard print versions of this book may not be included
in e-books or in print-on-demand. If this book refers to media such as a CD or DVD
that is not included in the version you purchased, you may download this material at
http://booksupport.wiley.com. For more information about Wiley products, visit
www.wiley.com.

Library of Congress Cataloging-in-Publication Data is Available

ISBN 978-1-118-85504-1 (Hardcover)
ISBN 978-1-119-04711-7 (ePDF)
ISBN 978-1-119-04703-2 (ePub)

Printed in the United States of America

10 9 8 7 6 5 4 3 2 1

To my clients, the source of inspiration and the real business heroes of this book.

To my husband, my partner, my friend, who believes in my dreams and helped me see who I am. And, who for years nagged me to write this book!

To my parents, who always told me that I could be anything that I wanted to be and I could do anything that I wanted to do.

My greatest pleasure is being a partner and catalyst in the success of my clients.

—Coach Vickie

Contents

Preface

To encourage you to think about your leadership behaviors and how those behaviors are affecting (negatively or positively) your performance, your authenticity, and your brand legacy is why I wrote this book. Too many leaders are so busy pursuing results that they do not even notice the wake of dead bodies in their path ... until it is way too late. Driving results is one aspect of leadership, and an important one, yet if you ignore the people side of driving results, your Inner Leader will never be able to emerge and thrive.

Each one of us has an Inner Leader that drives our performance, authenticity, and behaviors. My hope is that this book will help you open up the space to let the real leader in you show up. Once you become aware that your Inner Leader is yearning to escape, then you will be encouraged to take action.

Simply reading this book (thinking) without doing the exercises and trying on new behaviors (without action) makes your read only a cerebral experience. To maximize the results of your read; I encourage you to read the book, enjoy the case study stories, and commit to do the exercises, in whatever order or manner works for you.

The major concept in this book is that *anyone* can be a leader. Whatever the situation and with the proper tools, a leader can learn to recognize an opportunity and feel the confidence to let his or her authentic voice be heard. These lessons are useful for a variety of life's circumstances. The following people are all leaders: the most junior project manager who leads the company's global United Way campaign, the senior executive who coaches his son's Little League team, and the software developer who steps up in a program meeting with a suggestion that provides the needed focus to move forward. They are leaders because *they have the confidence to let their voice be heard and are comfortable influencing others to convert an idea from an abstract to an action.*

Unleashing your Inner Leader could mean anything. Analyzing everything that I have coached leaders on for the past 15 years was an interesting process. In all my joyful experiences with more than 4,000 coaching clients in 17 countries, there are some well-known concepts and techniques for leadership success that keep cropping up. My hardest task was organizing them into a meaningful book outline. This is because the coaching process is very dynamic. Time and time again, I would begin an engagement with a new client who would claim to want to be a better leader through improving his communication, and I would end up coaching him on personal branding. Or I would start with a stressed-out executive who got great results but whose family never saw her, and we ended up working on delegation. The book outline that finally emerged parallels the consistent themes that I have found to give the best return on investment (ROI) for my clients.

I wanted to reach a broader audience so that more leaders like you could find your authentic selves and begin to build your Leadership Legacies. In other words, I want to *maximize* a global group of leaders' potential. If this book gives readers at least one *aha* moment, or if they deploy one new behavior that changes the way that they lead, or they achieve a success that they never thought possible, then my mission will be realized.

About Me

One of my strengths is that I am a *maximizer*. This means that both in my corporate career in a high-impact industry and as an entrepreneurial executive coach, I like to take the good projects and make them great.

This discovery was a *huge aha* moment for me because it allowed me to target the projects that I wanted to work on—especially in my coaching practice. I learned that I only wanted to work with already successful people who want to get to the next level. Imagine how gratifying it is for me when I can honestly and authentically say to the person with whom I am working: *You* are my ideal client; you are smart and successful, and you want to be even more successful. Although it took me some time to figure this out, my return on investment (ROI) was huge. I now have no doubt about what I love to do and what I am good at. My Inner Leader is smiling.

My only measure of success is the success of my clients.

I am often asked who my business heroes are. My answer without hesitation is … my clients. Each of them was already successful, and because of some external or internal force, each needed to make a change. Together we worked tirelessly to bring that change to the forefront and make it happen. Changing human behavior is one of the most difficult tasks to accomplish. The personal changes that my clients have successfully made were hard to accomplish and yet they persevered. Their success has been unlimited and they are happy. This is why my only measure of success is the success of my clients because I know the hard work and dedication involved to get to their next step. Because of that hard work and dedication, they will forever be my business heroes.

About the Book

Are you excited to see what comes next? Are you ready to take on the challenges that await you in the following pages to make some very big changes in your leadership life? A cautionary question: What is going to be the biggest barrier to you making some of the changes suggested in the book? The answer is simple; change is *hard*. You might hear my suggested actions and think to yourself, "Oh yeah, I know that I need to do this, but (*you* fill in the blank) gets in my way of fully committing to take action." Remember that you did not get to this place of leadership by taking the easy road. These exercises will require the hardest thing for anyone to do, *to change your behavior from the inside out.*

Just as in my coaching practice, I am not going to let you off the hook so easily. I encourage you to act. Just as in a coaching engagement, doing the exercises in this book is critical. I have set them apart and made them easy to spot and understand. The exercises are designed to result in some learning and profound change for you.

While reading this book, I request that you take it a step further. For that special thing that you want to do this year, figure out what is holding you back and address it ... *head-on.* Pull on your Inner Leader and understand your values, strengths, skills, and past accomplishments to build a platform for future success. Drag all those positive attributes that you have kicking and screaming to center stage; let the world see what you can really accomplish. Who knows; you might even surprise yourself.

Acknowledgments

To all my clients, who have given me the joy of sharing in their personal journeys to unleash their Inner Leader. Your successes are my successes.

To my longtime friend Kelly Loy Morf, who believed in the book and found the opportunity for me to make it happen.

To Mary Charles Blakebrough, who painstakingly read and commented on almost every word.

To Alice Osborn, who helped me edit the original proposal for the book.

To Abby Weaver, for turning my ideas into great illustrations.

To all the people who read and commented on sections of the book, including Marguerite Lawn, Melissa Bennett, and Cheryl Pendergrass.

To the team at John Wiley & Sons and SAS for their editing, producing, and distribution support and for introducing me to the world of book publishing.

To all the individuals who shared their inspirational stories with me and in turn, with you, the reader.

To all the special people in my life who encouraged me during the writing process and constantly asked how it was going. Your support meant the world to me.

CHAPTER 1

You and Your Inner Leader

C oaching business professionals in high-impact industries to maximize their leadership performance is my expertise. This book is the culmination of the real-life experiences that my clients have faced: how they have unleashed their Inner Leader to live their legacies and develop into world-class leaders. The pages that follow are filled with real-life case studies, exercises, and personal stories that can help leaders like you to:

- Identify and leverage individual and team strengths to maximize performance
- Discover and understand how personal values drive your decisions and behavior
- Recognize and promote your career currency
- Take successful risks by discovering personal vision and purpose
- Build a personal brand and maximize both yours and the company's brand to make customers want to work with you
- Learn how to be more productive and how to delegate and empower your team

- Become a better mentor or mentee
- Communicate powerfully by improving your personal language
- Realize the power of networking to successfully evolve your career
- Understand how to better use the interview process to build a world-class team
- Determine and live your Leadership Legacy

Each chapter starts with a scenario (case study) based on a real client with whom I have worked (note that names have been changed to protect client anonymity). Each coaching session demonstrates an issue, challenge, or situation that the client has encountered. Based on this conversation, the pertinent parts of the situation are discussed and matched to a leadership concept. You are then engaged with powerful questioning that will prompt new thinking. The chapter continues with other examples of coaching sessions on related topics and with more discussion. Each chapter concludes with exercises that will help you incorporate this concept into your life. I highly recommend doing each of the exercises. It has been my experience that reading about a concept and thinking about it is the first step, and you will never make the desired change unless you take action and actually go through the steps to effect your own personal change. This is the recipe for lasting change that leads to success.

PART ONE OF THE BOOK

The book is organized into three parts. The first is dedicated to getting to know yourself. The concept being that leaders who are totally in touch with themselves and know what they are good at, what their vision is, and what impact they can make in their world; can begin to lead others and help others make their own impact.

In Chapter 2 you will meet Alexandra, who identified and leveraged her strengths to find her own voice. This then propelled her to negotiate a new position and then lead her new team from a position of strength. A strength is doing what you love to do and what you are good at. Once identified, you can leverage this to be happy in your career.

Understanding that your personal values are the rock that you stand on is one of the first tenets of leadership introduced in Chapter 3. When your environment is in sync with your values, you can produce your best work. When your values are being compromised, you are not on firm footing and your Inner Leader cannot shine through.

Chapter 4 will teach you how to recognize the impact that you have made in your organization. This is your career currency. Most people do not realize how much currency they truly have or how to spend it wisely within their organizations. When you learn how to promote the impact that you and your team have made, then others will understand your value to them and your career will evolve.

Building and maximizing your personal brand is the subject of Chapter 5. It is only once your vision, purpose, and goals become clear that you can begin to take successful risks with your career and your team. Your Inner Leader will have a guiding beacon for knowing what risks are right for you.

The exercises in Part One will be exercises for you to get to know yourself, which can sometimes be the hardest. Do not get discouraged; self-knowledge is an exciting self-discovery journey and essential to unleashing your Inner Leader. The case studies and the additional coaching stories are meant to illustrate the chapter concepts and give you *real-world* examples.

PART TWO OF THE BOOK

Part Two of this book is dedicated to the major topics that my clients have requested coaching on. Being more productive or doing more with less is always at the top of the list. Part of being more productive is learning how to delegate. Most leaders got to their current position by executing results. Once they find themselves in a position of leadership (whether formal or informal), letting go of the job and allowing others to do it is a very difficult thing. There are certain skills and techniques presented in Chapter 6, in the form of exercises to help you with being a successful delegator and improving productivity.

The next chapter is on mentoring. Mentoring is the most underrated key to leveraging your success. Mentoring is the relationship between two people in which there is mutual learning and sharing.

Developing yourself and your team into a world-class group of experts is what leadership is all about. This is the shortest chapter and in some ways the most powerful.

Communication is a leader's best friend, and the concept of examining your personal language is vital. As you will see in Chapter 8, many successful leaders sabotage themselves by using personal language that diminishes their success. You will learn to recognize powerful phrases and questioning techniques to communicate more powerfully.

Most leaders are so busy influencing results that they have little time for evolving their career. The only person whose job it is to evolve your career is *you*. In Chapter 9, you will learn about networking and interviewing. After driving results, when leaders come up for air, they realize that they do not have the appropriate skills to network effectively. Networking is the single biggest key to building your career because it is people who help you get promotions and new positions.

There is also a section on interviewing in Chapter 9. This might seem out of place in a leadership book, but being able to cut through the clutter and interview someone effectively (whether you are the interviewer or the interviewee) can ensure that you have the best people matched to the most important jobs in your organization.

Sustainability of strong leadership is the end goal to unleashing your Inner Leader. I call this *determining and living your Leadership Legacy*. Many of my successful clients came to me after a long (20-plus years) career, wanting more…wanting to follow their personal values and brand to still drive results, but in a more compassionate way. This is the time in their career that they want to *build and live* their Leadership Legacy. Chapter 10 will take the individuals from the case study in each chapter, which you will come to know, and extend their story to how they are currently living their Leadership Legacy.

PART THREE OF THE BOOK

The book's Part Three is a huge departure from the first two, in that it is a grouping of inspirational and motivating stories. There is nothing like hearing how "someone else did it" to help motivate and move us forward. While writing this book, I asked my community to share what inspires them. I received a large number of responses, which told me that inspiration was important to all. The inspirational stories are divided into the following categories:

- Guiding Principles
- Letting Go of *Me* to Get to *Us*
- Reflecting on the Past to Grow into the Future
- When *You* Are the Inspiration

In each of these categories the individual provides his or her inspiration and then tells the story of what makes this inspiration so important to them. It is amazing to feel all the changes that others have gone through and see the results of how they have handled their specific circumstances. In all these inspirational stories, having a clear goal for your behavior and your work gives clarity to living your Leadership Legacy.

HOW TO READ THIS BOOK

The way that you choose to read this book is, of course, up to you. If you want to read the whole book to get an overview and then go back and do the exercises, that is great. If you want to read it in spurts with the outcome of *you* immediately completing the exercises in each chapter, that is also a good strategy. The exercises will help you deploy the concepts and change your behavior within your leadership role. This is noted because the principles described in this book are about gaining unmistakable clarity about yourself to become a highly effective leader. I urge you not to gloss over the exercises but to truly commit to take the time to invest in yourself.

Another suggestion is to do the exercises with a friend, mentor, coach, or professional development group. A friend or mentor could be helpful while completing the self-knowledge exercises in Part One, because they know you well and could give you confirmation as you make self-discoveries. A coach or a professional development group could be helpful in discussing any of the techniques in Part Two with specific emphasis on changes in "process-oriented" personal interactions.

CHANGE MODEL: UNLEASHING YOUR INNER LEADER

Human behavior is one of the hardest things to change. Therefore, some of the exercises might be hard for you, because they are going to ask you to *change*. I tell the story of remodeling my kitchen. The trash container was moved five feet to the right of where it was previously. For more than a month, every time my husband and I went to throw something out, we literally went to the old spot. How ridiculous! My husband got furious with himself that he could not break such a simple habit. Yet, the research shows that you must consciously do something consistently for at least 30 days to build a new habit. Then, four months later, when I was especially stressed and went to throw something out, what did I do? You guessed it; I went to the "*old*" spot. The bottom line is that change is *hard,* and it takes a long time consistently implementing the new behavior for the change to become a constant.

I say this to encourage you to heartily embrace the changes discussed in the book and to understand that change is *hard*. Over the years I have built the following Change Model that I use for coaching, and it can also be used for any individual or organizational change (see Figure 1.1).

The first step is *Awareness*. Although the place where the awareness happens in each case study and chapter may be subtle, it will be found in every chapter of the book. As you read the case studies and concepts, begin thinking about your own life, and try to note how applicable this idea of awareness is for you. The exercises are designed to make this process easier and to ensure that you are very aware of the applicability of the leadership concept in your life. You might not

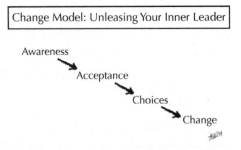

Figure 1.1 Change Model: Unleashing Your Inner Leader

be aware at first, and the exercises and case studies are designed to make you mindful of it.

The second step of *Acceptance* is much bigger than initially meets the eye. Say, for example, that you become aware that one of your underlying strengths is that you are extremely competitive. This is a great strength and should be used when right for the situation. You might have known this at some level before, but after doing the strengths exercises, you might find that this could actually be holding you back in certain instances. Accepting this fact may be difficult, and it is essential to you making a change to truly use your leadership powers and accept what you discover in the exercises.

The third step, *Choice*, might also be challenging for you. Earlier steps will show your awareness and personal commitment, which will in turn ensure your acceptance, but will you make the choice to change your competiveness? Are you truly ready to change that behavior by accepting that only by changing you will get to the next level of leadership? Congratulations to you when you make that choice. Then and only after you have gone through these first three steps will you be able to successfully make a lasting change in your leadership behavior.

The last step, *Change*, is the final goal. Once you have gone through the first three steps, you might think that change is easy, yet remember the moving of the trash can. Change takes lots of effort over time to really make it a part of you. By going through these first three steps, you can be clear that you have chosen the right change for you, and your change efforts will be highly rewarded.

ABOUT YOU

As you absorb case and client studies in the pages that follow, the exercises in the book will challenge you to recognize the opportunities to lead that you may have not recognized in the past. To that end, have you ever asked yourself something similar to one of these questions?

- Have I ever wanted to stand up and lead someone and did not?
- Have I ever left a meeting wondering why it was someone else who voiced the important point, when I was thinking the same thing all along?

- Have I ever been late in volunteering for a lead role, only to have it given to someone else?

- Have I ever been in the position to take a calculated risk and at the last minute decided against the move?

- Have I ever wanted to be a better leader and not known where to start?

If any of these situations resonate with you, then I would ask you the following questions: What made you hesitate? What got in your way?

As my years of coaching more than 4,000 business professionals in 17 countries shows, the answers have been as varied as the individuals and the industries that they work in. However, the resulting concept is always similar; everyone has a leader within him or her, and with some help, everyone can unleash that leader to become powerful and impactful. That is what this book will show you how to do—unleash your Inner Leader.

In Chapter 2, you will meet Alexandra. As you absorb her story, look for parallels from her experience to apply to yourself. Make the commitment to know yourself, understand your strengths and weaknesses completely, and find clarity about yourself and the value that you have to offer. Peeling back these layers will reveal for you that when you truly know yourself and you have unmistakable clarity on who you are and what your value is, then you become a highly effective business professional, and your Inner Leader will be unleashed.

YOU AND YOUR INNER LEADER CHAPTER SUMMARY

- This book is the culmination of the real-life experiences that my clients have faced: They have unleashed their Inner Leader to live their legacies and develop into world-class leaders.

- Part One is dedicated to getting to know yourself, because only when you know yourself can you begin to lead others and help others make their own impact.

- Part Two is dedicated to the major topics that my clients have requested coaching on: improving productivity, delegation, mentorship, personal language, networking, interviewing, and living your Leadership Legacy.

- Part Three is inspirational stories about guiding principles, letting go of *me* to get to *us*, reflecting on the past to get to the future, and when *you* become the inspiration.

- When you read this book, completing the exercises is essential. Whether you read it all the way through and then go back to do the exercises or do them as you read, I encourage you to actively participate in the exercises.

- Change is hard. To let your Inner Leader show through, you must be ready to make some changes to your behaviors, your actions, and potentially your beliefs.

- The Change Model consists of four steps: Awareness, Acceptance, Choice, and Change.

- After coaching more than 4,000 business professionals in 17 countries, the resulting concept is always similar: Everyone has a leader within them, and with some help, everyone can unleash their Inner Leader to become powerful and impactful.

PART
ONE

Know Yourself...
Authentically

Self-discovery is the key to unleashing your Inner Leader to the world. As shown in Figure 2.1, the first part of unleashing your Inner Leader is to know yourself...authentically. It is amazing that in all of the thousands of business professionals whom I have coached, they do not have clear answers to simple questions, such as:

- What are your top strengths?
- What do you value most?
- What is the most important impact that you make to your organization?
- What is your unique promise of value?

You can expect to discover the answers to these questions in Part One. I cannot emphasize enough the importance of completing the exercises in this part; they will give you the answers to catapult you to higher performance in Part Two. You can do them in any order, and the point is to *do* them all.

Go ahead; take the plunge into the pool of self-discovery. You will be one of the few leaders who really know themselves and then will be ready to unleash your leadership to the world!

CHAPTER **2**

Strengths:
Who Are You?

S uccessful leaders are adept at identifying and leveraging their strengths and those of their team. A strength is both what you love to do and what you are good at (your interests and your abilities). If you use your strengths in your job, you will gain clarity and get much more return on investment (ROI) on your personal energy. The secret to leadership transparency and authenticity is to find your three strengths and tell people about your strengths at least once a day; in six months others will use your words to describe you. A strength taken too far can be a weakness. You can leverage your strengths in career and professional development, succession planning, performance reviews, prioritizing work and time, and subtle promotion of self and group. Telling others your strengths is the first step to leadership transparency and authenticity; it allows your Inner Leader to emerge.

CASE STUDY

Meet Alexandra, a senior manager in the pharmaceutical industry. Alexandra is an introverted, empathetic genetic counselor who has worked very hard to get to the senior level. Her boss wanted to promote her to a director with 130 direct reports, but he refused to pay her the same compensation as her male predecessor. Because of her gentle nature, it was hard for her to ask for equal pay for an equal job done. That was before her leadership coaching.

Alexandra's story might seem, at first blush, like a simple case of convincing a manger or organization to offer fair pay for a certain level of responsibility. For Alexandra it was much more than that. She knew that she was a good leader and that her team thought so, but there were many times when her environment demanded that she be something that she was not—as she put it, "tough." I suggested that she begin an inward journey to fully discover what made her tick. In essence, she set out to discover her natural strengths. This chapter will help you do the same.

This chapter is dedicated to helping you build the life that you really want by asking you the questions: Does your life reflect who you are, and are you happy? The answer to these questions lies in understanding and knowing yourself; therefore, to build the life that you really want, you should consider:

- Discovering your natural strengths
- Leveraging your natural strengths
- Being confident enough in your authenticity (natural strengths) to let it drive your actions and behavior, even when you get stuck, want to quit, are stressed, or are figuring out what it is that you really want

We all have an inkling as to what makes us tick in general terms, for example: I am collaborative, not competitive; I am deliberative, not impulsive; I believe in action, not analysis; and I lead from the front. What I am asking here is for you to take the deep dive and go way below the surface to understand your innate strengths.

WHAT IS A STRENGTH?

Your strengths are your *who* and your results are your *what*. Everyone produces results. The differentiating factor is the impact of your results and *who* you are when you produce these results. The question becomes, Who are you when you are driving results? Asked a different way, how do you drive results? Imagine that I am looking for a new leader for a special project in my organization. Whether the hire is internal, external, or from my team whom I know very well, if I am looking for one type of leader, and I hire another type of leader, it will not be a good match for either side. As an example, if I am looking for the leader who drives results through building relationships with his or her team, but I hire the leader who drives results by sitting in an office analyzing data and asking his or her team to produce pounds of reports, neither the newly hired employee nor I will be happy. To use our strengths authentically, it is incumbent upon us to know ourselves intimately and show our strengths to the world.

When I was still working in the corporate world, trying to build the life that I really wanted, one of the important lessons that I learned from my coach, which I enthusiastically pass on in my coaching practice, is *identify your strengths—what you are good at and what you love to do. Then actively seek out environments in which you can use those strengths that make you the happiest.*

The diagram (Figure 2.1) that I use to demonstrate this shows your interests plus your abilities equals your strength.

Whenever I present this concept, I like to say that the whole game of being happy in your work is to *figure out what you are good at and what you love to do, and find someone to pay you to do it.*

As an illustration, I love to sing (interest), but I can clear a room because I am so bad (ability); and no one is going to pay me to do it. The point is that strengths must be both your interests and abilities.

The reason that this concept is so profound is because it can give you so much clarity.

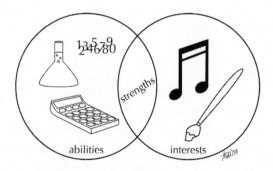

Figure 2.1 The Strength Formula

USING AND LEVERAGING YOUR STRENGTHS

The personal power that comes from being sure of what you are good at and what you love to do is the first step toward unleashing your Inner Leader. It certainly was a huge discovery for me. Remember the story told in Chapter 1? I discovered that I am a maximizer and that I am much happier working on the *good to great* projects rather than the *bad to good* projects. That has shaped my every decision and my every move forward. It almost becomes second nature to me that when I get a client referral, within the first 10 minutes of conversation, I can tell whether this is an ideal match for me or whether I should simply refer him or her to another coach whose strength is more in the *development* (bad to good) area.

This idea of finding clarity can be a huge boost to your productivity and efficiency. How, you might ask? The answer is that when you are doing what you love to do, it hardly feels like work; when you do more of what you love, you will become a master at it, and that will lead to ultimate success. Still not convinced? Let's think about the concept of spending your personal energy through the story of Carlton.

I worked with Carlton, a very successful project director whose top strength was harmony. What that meant for Carlton was that he led projects by moving all the stakeholders to consensus, and then he had to manage only the few exceptions that they could not agree on. Building consensus was his natural strength; he enjoyed leading in that mode and was good at what he did. Enter his new boss, who was extremely analytical and began to demand spreadsheet after spreadsheet from Carlton. Building spreadsheets was not Carlton's strength because he did not like it and he was not good at it. When Carlton came to me with this dilemma, we discussed the obvious. Maybe he could take some Excel classes and get better and more efficient at this task. Then I asked him the following question:

"What would be your personal return on this investment? For example, if you invest 50 percent of your time in this learning experience, will you receive at least an equal or greater return on your investment? In other words, if you invest 50 percent of your time in this, will you come out with at least 50 percent better Excel skills?"

Carlton rolled his eyes at me and emphatically stated that he hates building spreadsheets and no matter how many classes he attends, he knows that he would *never* get 50 percent better.

What would you do in this situation?

Much of Carlton's instinct was to grin and bear it and either wait for the boss to move on in a few years or leave the job that he used to love. I requested that he pull on his Inner Leader and think of other alternatives. The one he chose was simple: find someone on his staff who loves to do spreadsheets, who has a natural strength in analysis, and let him or her do it.

That seemed so simple but the person that he had in mind did not have building spreadsheets as part of his job. Carlton approached that person and they worked out a way to make this happen. Then Carlton used his natural strength of harmony (building consensus) and approached his boss, using his language of analysis. The boss not only hardily concurred that Carlton's staff person could do the spreadsheets but also was excited to have someone who loved building these spreadsheets to work with.

In today's world of doing more with less, this concept of personal return on investment is huge. However, it is usually at this point in the discussion that I get some interesting pushback. That pushback is normally in some form that states, "Vickie, this is all well and good, but my job is so demanding and so multifaceted that I just do not have the luxury of only doing what I love to do and what I am good at." My answer is that I understand that wholeheartedly, and my suggestion is that you slowly begin to chip away at parts of your work life where you can use your strengths. Imagine if you could make it a goal to use your strengths 20 percent of the time in the next four months. Then move on to expand that to using your strengths 30 percent in the following four months. Also, for those who are looking at the next step in their career, building a career plan around using your strengths could be exactly the secret ingredient that you have been looking for to help you find the place where you can do what you are good at and what you love to do and get paid for it. Now your Inner Leader will be smiling.

A word needs to be said here for those leaders who lead teams of people. Leading individuals with the concept of them using more and more of their strengths will help you build strong teams that are getting results and getting a much bigger return on their personal investment. How many of us have had an annual performance review where the boss spends 10 minutes telling us what we did well this year and the next 20 minutes talking about developmental items? Suppose that time or a true developmental discussion could center on what you do well, what you love to do, and what you would need to get even better at it. Wow!

STRENGTHS EXERCISE 1: DISCOVER YOUR STRENGTHS

The exercises in this book are pivotal to unleashing your Inner Leader. Here is the first.

One of the ways that I have developed to discover your strengths is to ask others with whom you have worked closely. These people could be colleagues, peers, bosses, subordinates, customers, and suppliers. Although this might seem a little weird, there are many ways in which you can couch your request. I have found that the simplest way is to say something such as, "I am embarking on a personal development plan and am requesting those people with whom I have worked closely to help me by answering the following question." Then you follow these steps:

Step 1 Survey your colleagues. E-mail 20 colleagues and ask them to respond to the question "What do you think are my three greatest strengths?" or put a different way, "If I asked you to describe me in three words or phrases, what would they be?"

Step 2 Once you receive the responses, ponder them carefully. You will have 60 words (20 × 3). Review all the words and group them into categories of like meanings. The groupings can be words that describe how you drive results, how you lead your team, your individual strengths, how you communicate, and so forth. From these groups, discover the three words that best describe you.

Step 3 Once you get your groupings and you have picked your top strengths, it would be helpful for you to share your 60 words with a few close individuals and ask them to help you narrow it down to three. Having a discussion with others could really help you pick the exact word that harnesses your strength.

Step 4 Remember the Change Model from Chapter 1? Take some time to build your own awareness of your words. For example, if one of your words is *ideas,* begin to notice real-life examples of when you deploy this strength. How many times do you think about different ideas in relation to your day-to-day job? Do people naturally come to you as the idea machine and do you deliver? To live your strengths each day, you should become very aware of real-life examples of how you do that. You will be surprised; as your awareness builds, you will begin to see situations where you might begin to change your behavior to be more in line with your strengths.

Discovering your strengths is not a check-the-box activity. You do not just get your three words and forget about them. As Figure 2.2 shows, the key to success in this activity is to make the commitment to use your three words, not simply to do the exercise and then forget it.

In 2001 Marcus Buckingham and Donald O. Clifton published a book, *Now, Discover Your Strengths* (Free Press). During that time the strengths wave hit many large corporations through their training and development departments. Whenever I go to one of these companies whose employees I know discovered their strengths, I make it a point to ask people what their strengths are. Sadly, 99 percent do not remember. That is because this exercise was simply a one-time deal with no follow-through. One resource is a book,

Figure 2.2 Discovering Your Strengths Is *Not* a Check-the-Box Activity

Strengthsfinder 2.0 (Gallup Press, 2007) by Tom Rath. Once you buy the book, either hardcover or electronic, you get a code, and you can go to www.strengthsfinder.com and take an assessment. The website will then send you a list of your top five strengths with a full report of definitions. Many of my clients have found this useful. Keep in mind that this is a result of only your input. Although I do heartily endorse using the www.strengthsfinder.com assessment to discover your strengths, I do it with two caveats. First, use it in combination with Strengths Exercise 1 so that you have a view from others as well as your view. Second, it is essential that you make a point to follow through and use your strengths as suggested in this chapter.

The suggestion is that your strengths are exactly that; they are unique to you and therefore should be used as the foundation to your authentic Inner Leader emerging throughout your career.

CASE STUDY

Alexandra completed Strengths Exercise 1 and discovered that her top two strengths were harmony and empathy. She was totally distraught as she told me these seemed to be the doormat strengths. She felt that she would never be able to stand up to anyone. I pointed out that those are exactly the strengths that made her a fabulous leader. Although she and her team certainly delivered results, her *who* was that she delivered results while always being able to see their side of the story and feel their pain. Alexandra committed to accept her strengths and figure out a way to use them to her advantage. Thus, she used her strengths of empathy and harmony to be the best leader that her group had ever had. With Coach Vickie's help, she also overcame, so to speak, those strengths when she had to fight for what she believed in both for herself and for others.

Another of my favorite strengths stories is of Adam who found himself in a career transition situation. He embraced the concept of discovering and leveraging his strengths to make sure that his next job was a good match for him and to ensure that he would excel.

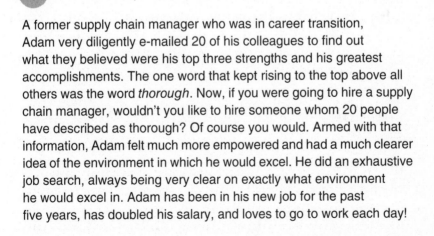

A former supply chain manager who was in career transition, Adam very diligently e-mailed 20 of his colleagues to find out what they believed were his top three strengths and his greatest accomplishments. The one word that kept rising to the top above all others was the word *thorough*. Now, if you were going to hire a supply chain manager, wouldn't you like to hire someone whom 20 people have described as thorough? Of course you would. Armed with that information, Adam felt much more empowered and had a much clearer idea of the environment in which he would excel. He did an exhaustive job search, always being very clear on exactly what environment he would excel in. Adam has been in his new job for the past five years, has doubled his salary, and loves to go to work each day!

This could be you! Discovering your authenticity is a gift that you can give to yourself. This is true whether you are looking to change jobs or simply to make your current position a bit more interesting; beginning to tell people what your strengths are is a great way to begin your authentic leadership journey.

Another of my favorite strengths stories is the following.

Eugenia is the former chief executive officer of a small financial firm who, in seven years, grew it by 300 percent and then successfully sold it (without any employee losing his or her job). After completing this exercise Eugenia determined that her biggest strength is that she is a "wall of positive energy." Armed with that and some great networking skills, she felt totally empowered and positively moved forward to the next step of her career. She started her own consulting firm so that her wall of positive energy can be the driving force for many other financial firms. Eugenia is excited to be doing what she loves to do and what she does well. In her first six months in business, she tripled her revenue projections!

Once you have identified your top three strengths, you are now ready for the next step in the process—*using* your strength words. Actively make them a part of your vocabulary. Consciously match your accomplishments with your strengths. Make it mandatory that you tell one person, each day, what you are good at. This can be very subtle, but over time the message will be clear.

STRENGTHS EXERCISE 2: BUILDING YOUR STRENGTHS STATEMENTS

Once you discover your strengths and choose three to five words that you have determined will be your message of who you really are, it is time to share them with *everyone* in your world. The best way that I have found to do that is to build a strength statement. That is a phrase of no more than a sentence that describes each of your strengths.

Once you build these strengths statements, you will be armed with the tools that you will need to tell others your strengths. Your strengths statements should be authentic and easy for you to say. They also should be very precise about describing who you are.

For Exercise 2 build a strength statement for each of your strength words that you have chosen to be the most descriptive of who you are. Write the strengths statements down and refine them until you believe that they are the most descriptive of you and that you are comfortable saying these statements to *everyone* in your world. Following are some examples to help you get started:

- Thank you; I was delighted to plan the event because *arranging* is one of my top strengths.
- Planning the event was a delight for me because I love being the *conductor* of a successful plan.
- I can help in this project by building the risk mitigation plan. I am very *deliberative* and once I examine all possibilities and build a plan, it will not unravel.
- I am a *maximizer;* I love to take good projects and make them great.
- I would like to lead the new project to get it up and running. I am an *activator;* I am good at taking action; my goal this year is to do more of it.
- I am the kind of person who loves to peer over the horizon to see what could be; some people call me *futuristic.*
- When people have input, the result is usually stronger. I encourage people to be *included* in the process. My motto is "If you want people to go to the mat for you, this happens only if they are *included."*
- I am a *maximizer;* I maximize employee and revenue potential.
- I am a *positive* person; I try to make work fun to have success in developing both employee and customer loyalty.
- My motto is that it is all about *relationships.* This helps me in developing strong bonds with my customers, which ultimately leads to increased revenue.

Was this exercise easy or hard? What made it worthwhile? Are you comfortable with your strengths statements? If so, move on to the next step; if not, go back and revise your statements until they are authentically you.

Why is it so important to say your words? There are many leadership concepts that talk about transparency and authenticity. Although those concepts seem like a good idea, I was never able to understand how to accomplish this. In my coaching practice I have seen firsthand how telling others of your strengths can help them better understand who you are and let your Inner Leader show through. Enabling others to understand *who* you are is the first step in leadership transparency and authenticity.

When I introduce the strength concept, I often get pushback, which mostly takes the form of people telling me that they were raised not to boast or that they have seen "chest beaters" in their life and do not want to be like that. My answer to these comments is to think about the fact that you are not boasting or chest beating, but rather, *you are concisely and precisely telling the facts about you*. You are simply stating transparently and authentically the facts about *who* you are.

For the past seven years I have been associated with a leadership program at the Corporate Education Center at Duke University. It is a one-week leadership program that global firms send their executives to from all corners of the world. The program includes individual coaching. Whenever I introduce the concept of sharing your strengths as a leader, I typically will hear the pushback "Vickie, that is okay for you Americans, but we [fill in the blank: French, Indians, Chinese, Brazilians, Nigerians, etc.] would never do that." It always makes me smile, because it seems that leaders from across the globe have a problem with transparency, even if it is concisely and precisely only telling the facts about themselves.

Now, if you can push through this seeming fear of telling others your strengths, it can be tremendously powerful. Here are the real results. If you can begin to tell others your strengths, guess what will happen. After a time, others will begin to describe you using your words. This is when your Inner Leader begins to emerge. As an executive coach, I have had many professionals in their thirties come to me, say that they want a promotion, and ask me to help guide them in this endeavor. A client of mine, Mario, in particular was very anxious to move up in his organization. The first questions that I asked him were:

- If I were to ask your boss to describe you in three words, what would he or she say?

- If I asked your boss's boss the same question, what would he or she say?

- If I were to ask your peers, your subordinates, your customers, and your suppliers the same question, what would they say?

If they all are not saying the same words, then you have not done your homework or the first step in your promotion plan.

STRENGTHS EXERCISE 3: COMMUNICATING YOUR STRENGTHS STATEMENTS

Now that you have written your strengths statements, Exercise 3 is simple; it is to *say a strength statement to someone in your world at least once a day.* What is the reason behind this? Just like Carlton, Adam, Eugenia, and Alexandra, *you* have to be so comfortable with talking about your strengths that the words will come in a time of crisis; or they will come when that person of influence gets on the elevator, and you have 10 seconds to begin a conversation. If he or she likes what you say, the conversation will continue. As mentioned earlier, it is hard to get started telling others what your strengths are. Please power through the first few weeks of discomfort; it is important for your Inner Leader to show itself in this authentic manner. After a few months, when you get the rewards of others describing you using your words, the difficulty of changing your behavior will be worth it.

CASE STUDY

After Alexandra worked with me for eight months, she discovered her strengths and got comfortable saying her strengths statements and leveraging her strengths. Then guess what happened—*she found her own voice*. This was huge for her. It made her feel powerful and confident. Alexandra answered her boss's objections in an authentic way that felt right for her. The specific method she used when he brought up her promotion was to hold up her hand and have this prepared one-sentence statement: "When you are prepared to pay me equally, we can have this conversation." Because of her action, Alexandra got the pay she deserved and worked in this position for two years.

WHEN STRENGTH BECOMES A WEAKNESS

There is one last point to make regarding discovering and leveraging your strengths. That point is that a strength, taken too far, can be a weakness. That is a little sentence with a big punch. When you overuse or take a strength to the extreme, it can be a detriment or a weakness. An example is competitiveness when taken to the extreme; means winning at all costs. Or if someone is an activator, this is the *fire, ready, aim* person; taken to an extreme, nothing is ever finished, but there are a million projects started. Or when someone who is extremely analytical overuses this strength, it can lead to needing more information constantly before making a decision (analysis paralysis).

As you can see, we need to build some awareness around us overusing our strengths and build in some personal management of this behavior. If you are truly trying not to overuse a strength, I strongly suggest that you find a trusted confidant who will give you honest feedback, preferably in the moment, so that you can pull back your behavior. This is also potentially a way for a manager to give feedback to a subordinate who is very good and sometimes overuses his or her strengths.

When we get into a stress mode, this can be even more exaggerated. When we are stressed, we go into the mode that has always served us well in the past. So if you have the strength of achievement, you become the total workaholic because this is your natural strength. If you have the strength of responsibility and you are in a stressed environment, you will take on everyone else's piece of the project to make sure that all the deliverables are met even if they are not yours. If you have the strength of communication, taken to the extreme, you will overcommunicate to the point that no one can get any work done because you are so busy communicating. Do any of these behaviors resonate with you, or do you have colleagues that you recognize in this scenario?

Once again, the first step toward making the change to discover your Inner Leader is to build awareness. By this I mean build awareness of the person you are when you are using your strengths and what behaviors using your strengths drives. Remember the golden rule: When you do what you are good at and what you love to do, you will be happiest, and your leadership will be authentic and transparent.

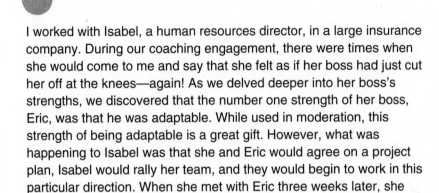

I worked with Isabel, a human resources director, in a large insurance company. During our coaching engagement, there were times when she would come to me and say that she felt as if her boss had just cut her off at the knees—again! As we delved deeper into her boss's strengths, we discovered that the number one strength of her boss, Eric, was that he was adaptable. While used in moderation, this strength of being adaptable is a great gift. However, what was happening to Isabel was that she and Eric would agree on a project plan, Isabel would rally her team, and they would begin to work in this particular direction. When she met with Eric three weeks later, she did not even recognize what he was talking about. He was so adaptable that he had followed another path. This was a huge *aha* moment for both Eric and Isabel. Once Eric learned how to manage this strength of being adaptable, he kept his desire to follow the next great idea at bay. This enabled Isabel and her team to follow the agreed-upon direction and complete the project. It also made Eric a much better boss once he understood that he had been overusing his strength of adaptability.

Note that I follow and admire Marcus Buckingham, who is sometimes called the father of the strengths movement. Although he has written many books, I have found two books, *Strengthfinder 2.0* (Tom Rath, Gallup Press, 2007) and *Strength Based Leadership: Great Leaders, Teams, and Why People Follow Them* (Tom Rath and Barry Conchie, Gallup Press, 2009), valuable resources to augment your strengths work.

As you have read the concepts in this chapter, has Alexandra come to mind? She actively embraced many of the concepts presented and had some hard-fought conversations with her Inner Leader to be able to move to the life that she really wanted and to find her own voice. By way of a summary of the chapter, Alexandra ...

CASE STUDY

Discovered and accepted her strengths and figured out a way to use them to her advantage. Did she get stuck? Absolutely. Did she stumble when she discovered that she had to influence her boss to do the right thing? Absolutely. Was it hard? Absolutely. Did she find support and pull on her coach? Absolutely. Once she found her own voice, her world began to change. Because of her actions, Alexandra got the pay that she deserved and worked in this position for two years. When she left this job, her team gave her a diamond necklace! Now she is working her dream job—but not for long, because the one thing that she knows for sure is that she will continue to grow and make an impact in the genetics world. In fact, the first two lines of her professional biography say it all: "Alexandra is acclaimed as a leader, role model, and visionary in the genetics field. She is recognized for her ability to see the larger picture and envision the possibilities for improving patient care."

This story happened five years ago. Currently, when I speak with Alexandra, she is still happy with her life and knows that it is because she found her own voice. She figured out what makes her happy and found a working environment that fit her very well. By diligently doing the exercises presented in this chapter, she increased her awareness of the strengths that she did have, she actively managed the times that she had to step out of her comfort zone, and she embraced *who* she authentically is to unleash her Inner Leader and lead transparently.

The gift that she gave her former team was that they began to embrace and leverage their strengths by her example. Since then several members of Alexandra's team have moved on. The best praise that she has ever gotten was when one of her former teammates landed a great new job in a company where the corporate environment was a good match for this individual's strengths, and this teammate told Alexandra that her new boss in her new company was just like Alexandra.

STRENGTHS CHAPTER SUMMARY

- A strength is what you love to do and what you do well.

- If you use your strengths in your job, you will gain clarity and get much more return on your personal energy.

- A strength taken too far or overused is a weakness and must be managed.

- Exercise 1: To discover your strengths, ask 20 colleagues how they would describe you, and then cull the results down to three words.

- Exercise 2: Develop and say your strengths statements at least once a day so that in six months your team will use your words to describe you.

- Exercise 3: Develop a personal awareness of when you best leverage your strengths, and resolve to do more of that. The goal is to use your strengths more than 30 percent of the time in your work.

- Telling others your strengths is the first step to leadership transparency and authenticity; it allows your Inner Leader to emerge.

CHAPTER 3

Values: What Do You Stand For?

uccessful leaders are adept at identifying and leveraging their values. Your values are the rock that you stand on. When your values align with your environment, you will behave in your most authentic manner and your Inner Leader can emerge. The opposite is true. When your values are compromised, you are not on firm footing and your Inner Leader cannot shine through. The benefit to understanding and living your values is that you get clarity and a positive return on your expenditure of emotional energy. If something does not feel right, it is probably because it violates your values. You need to live your values and align them to your behavior. Your behavior is a reflection of your values. When your values, environment, and behavior align, you are inviting your Inner Leader to emerge.

CASE STUDY

Meet David, an executive in the software industry. He came from a military background and was known in his company for getting things done. For 12 years he had been rewarded very well for the results he produced. Now that he was the highest-ranking individual at his regional site, he was told that he needed to be more of a leader. When he came to the coaching engagement, not only was he confused by the company's current feedback on him, but also for the first time in his 20-year career, he was confused on what his next step should be. In fact with his quick wit, he characterized his situation as "For the last 12 years I have been the 'fix it' guy. What does being more of a leader mean? Maybe now they want me to say *please* before I turn bad situations into good ones?"

Have you ever been in a situation like this? Have you ever had a colleague, boss, or subordinate in a situation like this? What did you tell him or her? Sometimes the most important analysis to a personal business issue is to really discover what the root cause is. When I, as a coach, come to a new engagement, I come with my bag of tools that consists of a multitude of 360-degree feedback instruments, exercises that are targeted toward specific aspects of leadership, my listening skills, and intuition. In David's case, he was highly educated (he had a PhD in leadership—what was I going to teach him?); he had a high level of emotional intelligence, or stated another way, he was much attuned to the needs of others. So what was the real root of the problem here?

In most leadership coaching engagements, I will typically start with the strengths exercises and then move on to do a values exercise. Why? Because in my mind these are the most personal aspects of leadership. To explain, let me ask the question...

WHAT IS A VALUE?

This is *not* a rhetorical question. Please stop reading and answer the question. It is important to really think about what your definition of a value is and what it means to you. When I ask this question in an individual coaching session or in a workshop venue, many times I will get answers such as:

- Values are what you believe in.
- A value is what is important to me.

- Values are your guiding principles.
- A value is the rule that I live by.

These are all correct. The definition that I like to use is that a value is *the rock that you stand on*. It is your foundation; it is what keeps you grounded.

To let your Inner Leader emerge, you need to be very sure of your values. If you are standing on solid ground, then you can lead others. However, what sometimes happens is that your values rock will begin to be chipped away at. Without you even realizing it, external forces will begin taking pieces of your rock away until one day you realize that you have only one part of one foot on your rock, and you are suddenly feeling like you are standing on very shaky ground. Has this ever happened to you?

Figure 3.1 A Value Is the Rock That You Stand On

Figure 3.2 Are Your Values on Shaky Ground?

VALUES DRIVE DECISIONS AND BEHAVIORS

Values are your own personal global positioning system (GPS); they are the operating system of your beliefs. Values drive your decisions because you will naturally align with the direction that is part of your value system. Also when your values align with your external environment, it leads to personal fulfillment. Think back to the best job that you ever had—there was probably a lot of alignment with your environment (boss, department, team, company, project, and coworkers). This alignment leads to personal fulfillment, and that leads to your behaving in a more authentic manner that enables your true leader to emerge.

The opposite is also true—bothersome events occur when values are violated. Uncomfortable situations arise when our values are being violated. Certainly we can think about the big situations, such as when a stakeholder asks you to make a decision that is illegal, immoral, or just plain wrong. Yet many times the situation can be a lot less clear. For example, when a stakeholder asks you to make a decision to take the project, division, or team in a slightly different direction than you would have taken, this is when the rock that you stand on begins to be chipped away at.

At other times your values might be violated, but you cannot even determine what is wrong or what is bothering you. My general rule is that when you are usually emotional about an issue or a situation, your values are potentially being violated. This is because values are so close to our core that when big pieces are chipped off our rock, we will become much more emotional about it because our values are so important.

Horace is a nurse by education and early experience who ran a human immunodeficiency virus (HIV) clinic for 10 years. He personally witnessed the intimate struggles that his patients had finding the appropriate treatment to help them retain their dignity while fighting the disease. Horace discovered that he wanted to play on a bigger scale and to have a larger impact. He went to work for a global pharmaceutical company that was the leader in HIV treatments. His passion eclipsed his dedication and Horace became very successful. I met him during a training workshop that I did at his company. Part of the workshop was on values (including exercises). Employees were enlightened about matching their values to their work environment to find true happiness. I also mentioned my concept that if you become emotional about a work issue, chances are that some of your personal values are being violated. In the back of the room, a dark cloud came over Horace's face. Later that day I had an opportunity to ask him what he had been thinking at that moment. His answer was:

> Vickie, I am so passionate about what I do and I am in the correct environment for me that I am always in harmony with my job and my colleagues. But when you made the statement about getting emotional about a work issue and that the source of frustration could be that values are being

violated, that really resonated with me. Last year for the first time in my life, I was not happy at work and it affected everything that I did. I almost thought of quitting this great company that I work for. You now have given me the clarity that I needed. At that time the values of my boss did not match with my values. Wow, that is a huge lesson for me and I am glad that I changed jobs and did not quit.

WHEN VALUES ARE MISALIGNED

At this point your natural instinct might be to ask what to do about a situation where values are misaligned. My answer would be to remember the Change Model introduced in Chapter 1 (reproduced here as Figure 3.3).

The first step to any change is awareness, and the first step to unleashing your Inner Leader is self-awareness. I am not asking you to change your values; I am asking you to become extremely self-aware and aware of what is going on around you. The challenge is for you to really delve into what your top values are and how these values show up in your life. This essential exercise will lead to personal leadership discoveries. Once you know your values and have accepted your values, then you can begin to see what choices you have and can make. Finally when you make a change to the situation, you can feel comfortable that your decision was the right one for you and the situation.

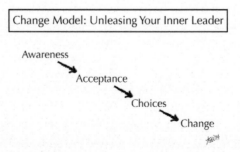

Figure 3.3 Coach Vickie's Change Model

Because David's dilemma was about his leadership behavior, I did not start with strengths or values, but we did two leadership 360-degree feedback exercises with him and his team. Interestingly enough, through doing these exercises one thing jumped out that nearly knocked us both over. Because of his upbringing and background, it became clear that David had a huge sense of *duty*. Put another way, his number one value was duty. Now we can all say that we feel a sense of loyalty, duty, and pledging in our lives but for David it was overwhelming. He had lived by this golden rule for his whole life. What is wrong with that, you ask? Nothing, except that in today's business world such a strong sense of duty above all else was getting in David's way. He took some months to accept this value and to see how overwhelmingly powerful it was in his life and how he now had some choices to make.

When discussing strengths, we said that knowing your strengths gives you clarity and helps you manage your personal energy. Doing more of the things that you love to do and do well will give you a much greater return on your personal energy expenditure. This will in turn make you a much more productive and effective leader. The key to understanding and living your values is also clarity and the positive return that you get on your expenditure of your *emotional* energy. How many times have you rolled around in your head a business situation that you were emotional about, with no new conclusions? How many times have you discussed a performance issue with other colleagues and never gotten to make a decision? The next time that a situation is gnawing at you, after you consider all the facts and you are still having a hard time making the decision, I would invite you to turn to the values side of the equation, just as Horace did. There are many times when your values will not be in alignment with others; that is when the awareness and acceptance steps are highly important for you to make the correct choice.

I am often asked whether values change over time. The answer is no; we are hardwired to the rock that we stand on. In David's case his sense of duty will never change; it is how he is hardwired. Horace will always value the accomplishment of a goal and that will never change. Values are internal motivators that will drive our behavior. There is a caution here. Values can sometimes be confused with needs, which are also motivators. Needs are very different from values. For example, a young professional might need a high level of business risk more than someone who is about to retire. A person with many family obligations might need benefits much more than a person with no family obligations. This is where the line between values and needs begins to get blurry. I suggest that when you do the values exercises below, you think hard about whether this is a value or a need.

I spent 7 years of my coaching career working part-time as a career coach for the local office of Right Management. I worked with the executive candidates who had been let go from their jobs. During this time the economy had swings from terrible to good and back to bad. Certainly the worse the economy was, the harder the job search was for some of these very successful veterans of high-impact jobs. One of the first questions that I would always ask an executive was, What are your top four criteria for your next job? The answers that I got were amazing, and they could be categorized into two themes. One was very *needs* oriented and it sounded like this: I need to make X dollars, have benefits for my family, travel a maximum of 25 percent of the time, and use my master of business administration that I recently got. The other was very *values* oriented and sounded like this: I have lots of experience in X industry, and I would like to lead a team where I can mentor it to make a bottom line impact while helping each team member grow professionally. Those are very different perspectives and both are important to be a good leader. For this chapter and its exercises, the focus is still on values and discovering and accepting the rock that you stand on.

By way of illustration, the first time that I did my values exercises, I asked a trusted colleague to help me. We had a good discussion until it came down to one word. He believed that I was controlling. *Wow,* that shocked and almost hurt me. When I asked him to give me examples, together we began to realize that it wasn't that I was controlling; it was that I really value order in my life. Some of you may laugh, but after a business trip, I come home, spend five minutes with my family, and then have to unpack. It normally takes me only 10 minutes, but until I get my order taken care of, I am not fully present for my family. What this has made me realize is that any kind of change is messy, so when I am getting ready to face a big change in my personal or business life, it really helps me to have the rest of my life in order.

Now let's take this knowledge to the office. Suppose as a leader I have let my team know of my value of order. How does this help you understand me? Well, if you come into my office or workspace with the intention of asking for a raise, and my desk is a disaster, do you think that this is a good time to have this particular conversation?

Once again, knowing your values drives clarity and return on your emotional energy. On to values exercises: I have been working with values for more 15 years, and in all that time I have believed that there is only one way to truly discover one's own values. That is to look at a list of words and to begin to decide what *your* values are. Being the maximizer that I am, I have never felt the need to make up my own values exercise. There are many of them. I am therefore using the list in the following section from the Reach Company, a fabulous company through which I am certified.

VALUES EXERCISE 1: DISCOVER YOUR VALUES

Look at the list of words below, and choose the top 15 that you resonate with. Then go through those 15 and get them down to three to five values. You should then give the list of words to at least two people who know you very well; one could be a spouse, family member, or friend, and the other could be a coworker or colleague. Have them go through the same exercise for you and then share their thought patterns with you. For example, what top 15 did they pick for you, and what were your behavioral examples that they used to get your list down to three to five values? You might be surprised at what others see in you versus what you see in yourself.

Accessibility	Courage	Growth	Prosperity
Accomplishment	Creativity	Harmony	Punctuality
Accountability	Curiosity	Health	Realism
Accuracy	Dependability	Honesty	Recognition
Adaptability	Determination	Honor	Relaxation
Adventure	Devotion	Humor	Reliability
Affection	Dignity	Imagination	Resourcefulness
Affluence	Directness	Impact	Respect
Altruism	Discipline	Independence	Security
Ambition	Diversity	Integrity	Self-control
Assertiveness	Efficiency	Intelligence	Sensitivity
Balance	Elegance	Justice	Significance
Belonging	Empathy	Kindness	Sincerity
Bravery	Endurance	Knowledge	Speed
Calmness	Enthusiasm	Leadership	Spirituality
Celebrity	Excellence	Learning	Spontaneity
Challenge	Experience	Love	Stability
Charity	Expertise	Loyalty	Strength
Clarity	Fairness	Mindfulness	Structure
Cleverness	Faith	Optimism	Success
Comfort	Fame	Originality	Support
Commitment	Family	Passion	Sympathy
Compassion	Fidelity	Peace	Teamwork
Completion	Flexibility	Perfection	Understanding
Conformity	Frugality	Perseverance	Virtue
Contentment	Fun	Persuasiveness	Vision
Control	Generosity	Power	Wealth
Conviction	Grace	Precision	Winning
Cooperation	Gratitude	Professionalism	Zeal

How did that exercise feel? Was it fun, hard, exciting, or enlightening? Were your initial words very different from the ones that your colleagues and friends picked for you?

VALUES EXERCISE 2: ALIGN YOUR VALUES AND BEHAVIOR

Now that you have identified your values, spend some time, at least a few weeks, working with them. For example, take your three to five values and measure them on a scale of 1 to 10 in terms of how much in alignment your current life is with your values. Then for each of your values, review the steps below or think in your own way about how you can increase the alignment of your values with your daily life.

Step 1   Identify examples or situations when you feel you are using your values.

Step 2   Identify situations when you feel that your values do not align with them.

Step 3   When you find alignment, how do you behave? Is this the behavior that most reflects your values?

Step 4   When you find misalignment, how do you behave? Is this the best behavior for this situation, or now that you understand your values, is there a better behavior that you could try?

What did this exercise show you? Hopefully it demonstrated that alignment of values with the many facets of your life is critical to your success and to unleashing your Inner Leader. Are your values well aligned with those of your organization, your department, your boss, your peers, your subordinates, your friends, and your colleagues? It is critical to your career success that there be alignment in your life. Also, here is a note to leaders who might be dealing with individuals in their department who are not performing to objectives. Take a tip from Horace and spend some time analyzing not just the business facts; have a discussion on what this person truly values. If you are in a mentor relationship (as either the mentor or the mentee), suggest a discussion on values. If you are in a leadership position and you have professional development or succession planning responsibilities, remember to include a piece of your discussion on values.

CASE STUDY

David began to realize that his *deep* sense of duty was a weakness for him. He thought about some past performance reviews that he had given. Had his sense of duty skewed his thinking? Was there anyone as committed as he was? He used to take pride in that, and now he realized that his sense of duty was probably making him overbearing in many scenarios. David's awareness and acceptance enabled him to make the choice to change his behavior. This behavior change started in his head with the motto *okay work was good enough*. The way that he implemented this change is that he made a decision to suggest his idea once, and if it was not taken, he would not try to shove it down someone's throat. Although this change was tremendously hard for him, he finally found some peace and actually became a better leader. The way that he supported his team demonstrated much of his outward change. He realized that he needed to support his team the way *it needed* to be supported, not the way *he felt* he needed to support it. Coach Vickie calls this living the platinum rule—treating others the way that *they need* to be treated, not the way that *you feel* they need to be treated.

VALUES CHAPTER SUMMARY

- Your values are the rock that you stand on.

- When your values align with your environment, you will behave in your most authentic manner and your Inner Leader can emerge. The opposite is true.

- When your values are compromised, you are not on firm footing and your Inner Leader cannot shine through.

- The benefit to understanding and living your values is that you get clarity and a positive return on your expenditure of emotional energy.

- If something does not feel right, it is probably because it violates your values.

- Values Exercise 1: Discover and accept your top three to five values.

- Values Exercise 2: Develop a plan to have maximum alignment of your values with your environment (boss, department, team, company, project, and coworkers). In other words, do your values match those of your environment?

CHAPTER 4

Impact: What Do You Do?

S uccessful leaders are adept at communicating their impact and the impact of their team to anyone, anytime, anywhere. Communicating your accomplishments in the CAR (Challenge, Action, Result) format is the technique that successful leaders use to demonstrate their impact. Your CAR stories are your *career currency*, or the foundation upon which you build your career. CAR stories can be successfully used in performance reviews and introductions to communicate your impact to the organization concisely. You can also match your CAR stories to company leadership competencies when writing performance reviews.

CASE STUDY

Meet Edward. He had worked for one of the top global technology companies for the past 12 years. Although he had had many successes, he felt as if his career had simply been "floating along." He had changed jobs four times with simply the average salary bump and only one promotion. When he came to work with me, his goal was very clear; it was time to become more serious about his career and to work actively on getting his accomplishments noticed so that he could get some real promotions. He had no idea how to do this.

GET YOUR RESULTS NOTICED

In this chapter you will learn the techniques to get your accomplishments noticed, and you will see how Edward implemented these practices. Let's get started with a story.

I recently did a presentation at a local high-tech company. I began by asking the audience the following question: *Of those people who you work closely with (your peers, subordinates, bosses, customers, suppliers, stakeholders), how many of them truly know what successes or accomplishments you have had this year?*

The question seemed to stop them cold, and I had some stunned faces staring back at me. In my years of coaching this has been a common response to this question. It always surprises me that I work with some incredibly talented people who are doing some amazing things, and yet no one in their world seems to recognize their impact, or better said, their value, to the organization.

Why is it that others around you do not know the incredible things that you have done for your organization? The answer of course, just like Edward, is that you probably have rolled along in your job, getting small recognitions and potentially some job changes yet no *big* recognition. What is holding you back? Do you want to change this? Then read on.

Typically when the subject of others knowing what your successes are comes up, I get several comments, the first of which is something like "Vickie, shouldn't my accomplishments be enough? I always believed that my actions would speak for themselves. After all, what is that old saying—actions speak louder than words? Isn't it my boss's job to know what I am doing?" All of this may be true, but the reality is that most of the people whom you work with are so imbedded in their own work that they really do not know much of anything else around them, in any detail. Another reality is that your boss may be in another location or perhaps even another country.

The second comment that is often raised during my presentations is fear of the bad effects of self-promotion. In the same presentation referenced earlier, I asked for the feelings that come up when I say the word *self-promotion*. The list included bragging, arrogant, selfish, egotistical, and chest-thumping. So then the issue really becomes, Are you proud of your successes and accomplishments? If the answer is yes, then the conclusion is that you simply have to learn how to communicate your impact to your organization in a manner that is comfortable for you and in a manner in which others will hear you. Simple enough—so let's get started.

IMPACT EXERCISE 1: BUILD YOUR CAR STORIES—CHALLENGE, ACTION, RESULT

In this chapter, the first exercise will come early because it doubles as the technique by which you can communicate your accomplishments in a logical, factual, and impactful manner:

1. Make a list of your top 20 successes. This could be from your entire career, it could be from your last two positions, or it could be in the past seven years. Whatever time frame you pick, select your most impressive accomplishment. The way you note your list can be anything that will jog your memory: for example, working with Sam, project ABC, or customer X's implementation.

2. Once you have made the list, write out the story of this success, using the following format: Challenge, Action, Result. These stories will become known as your CAR stories. The Challenge is, What was the problem, issue, or situation that you were trying to solve or affect? The Action is, Exactly what action did you take? The Result is, your impact on the problem and the benefits that the organization received from this impact; it *must* include a number.

3. Once you have written out the story for each of these 20 successes, go back to each story, and edit out all the unnecessary words and phrases so that you can tell the entire story in just five sentences.

A few words about this exercise: First, it is hard. I sincerely request that you push yourself and pull on any resources that you have to get this done. Second, if you define the challenge well, then the result will be easier. For example, if the challenge is to automate a process to reduce the time it takes to complete the process to get invoices paid, then the result will be "reduced the invoice payment process from 60 days to 15 days." Another example could be the challenge of reducing costs in the next year by 10 percent. Still another could be increasing sales leads by 30 percent in the next 6 months.

The secret to writing powerful CAR stories is to be as specific as possible, which usually means defining the components by numbers. I get lots of pushback on this point initially, and it sounds like this: "Vickie, I am just one step in the overall software development process. I do my coding and then I send it to the next developer." My answer is that you need to push yourself. Typically a developer's goal is on-time delivery with zero defects. How close do you come to meeting this goal? If you have not been measuring that before, you need to start measuring that now.

The other pushback that I hear is "I am part of a huge project team. We have over 100 people working to implement this global project, and my part is small." For this concern there are two answers. First, you still have specific objectives that you are responsible for delivering; try to break those down into the CAR formula. For example, if you are responsible for managing outside vendors on the project and the entire project has the goal of reducing costs by 10 percent, then you can talk about what you did to contribute to the project goal.

The second answer falls into a larger category of individuals allowing themselves to claim the result of the entire project as their own. I always have individuals say that they cannot claim the $2 million brought in the first two months of the new product launch (which was double the projected $1 million) because it was the effort of the whole team. Some people feel that their part, although important, was small, and therefore they cannot claim the entire project's result as their own. It is here that a sports analogy is of great use. Isn't it true that even the injured player who sits out half of the season still gets the Super Bowl ring? Yes, because he was part of the winning team. Look at the back of a baseball card; it not only shows individual statistics, but it also shows team statistics. This is because that player is part of the team, and he owns, so to speak, the team statistics. Even the junior assistants on the hockey team get to be part of the celebration when they win the Stanley Cup. So why do we not believe that our part of the large project was not enough to contribute to the larger business success?

Thinking back to the Change Model in Chapter 1, the first step to change is Awareness of your accomplishments. The second step is Acceptance, accepting the fact that you have impactful successes and that it is incumbent upon you to let others in your organization know about your impact. That acceptance will take some time, some thinking, and some discussion, and hopefully these exercises will lead you to a huge paradigm shift. Think about what it is that *you* need to make the major shift and begin to describe your successes in the CAR format. Human change is not easy, but the results are worth it.

Here are several examples of CAR stories my clients wrote; I hope that they inspire you to write yours.

Opening the Raleigh office from scratch (example of business development)

Challenge: Expanding a staffing business that was western New York based only, to a new region of the country from the ground up.

Action: After researching areas to expand, the Raleigh office was opened in October 2001.

Result: Thirteen years later in 2014, the Raleigh office was ranked eleventh among over 200 staffing firms in the area. The office had four people generating $2.2 million in revenue.

Creating the 2010 bonus program (example of sales management)

Challenge: Create a bonus plan that would motivate individuals while also nurturing the team concept of 15 sales and recruiting individuals.

Action: Developed a plan that distributed shares in the bonus plan based on position. These shares were then used to divide the profit that was generated by the team. A trip bonus was also attached for the overall performance.

Result: The trip bonus was achieved and revenue increased by 5 percent (2 percent above projected results).

Partner with the customer to develop a training program to reduce turnover (example of customer satisfaction)

Challenge: Turnover in the manufacturing floor for temporary employees was close to 70 percent. This was due to inexperience with the machines and unfamiliarity with the work environment.

Action: Since my agency was providing the temporary employees, I developed a 2-week training program that included classroom and hands-on training, facilitated by both the agency and customer employees.

Result: After a 6-month period turnover among manufacturing temps was below 5 percent. There was also increased customer satisfaction by 75 percent with the agency's services of providing these temporary employees.

Automation of advertising tracking code database (example of using automation to improve productivity)

Challenge: The manual processes involved in managing the tracking codes and phone numbers used by the advertising teams caused inaccuracy, customer dissatisfaction, and the potential loss of sales along with being time-consuming.

Action: Spearheaded the creation of a Web portal front end for users to submit requests, receive approvals, and track progress of key codes and phone numbers during the setup process that was linked to our customer database where the administrator could use automated feeds and processes to approve behind the scenes.

Result: The automation of this database improved productivity by 67 percent by reducing 3 weeks of work per month down to 1 week, saving 24 weeks a year, and increased accuracy, communications, and client satisfaction for the 45 clients who used this service. In addition, the automated environment also supported the creation of summary reports on the Web that helped users manage and organize the 1,800 advertising codes and 300 phone numbers moving in and out of the market.

Strategic supply chain analysis for storage products (example of increasing supply chain efficiencies)

Challenge: Develop and maintain an effective global supply chain that meets the requirements of competitive terms and conditions, product quality standards, logistic requirements, and delivery time-lines, with aggressive cost reduction targets in an environment of hyper growth and competition.

Action: Analyzed the potential supplier base on product road maps, financial positioning, and strategic opportunities that were used to create insights and recommendations for the senior management team to consolidate suppliers and increase strategic leverage.

Result: The storage supply base was cut down by over 50 percent from 19 suppliers to 9 strategic partnerships. This vendor reduction also reduced the time to manage these suppliers. This time saving was used to offset the increased demands caused by the increased growth in product shipments of 80 percent over two years, so the net gain was we were able to sustain the current staffing levels.

Programmer service improvement (example of reduction of time to complete a deliverable)

Challenge: A careful analysis of our "first come, first serve" application development service proved to hold small projects of 15 hours or less in the work queue an average of 37 business days.

Action: I developed a process to classify programmers' technical skill levels (beginner, intermediate, or advanced), and to classify projects based on complexity, allowing assignment of projects' technical complexity to programmer skill levels.

Result: Seventy-six percent reduction in time to complete a small development project, leading to a formal process change, an award as the "Best of Best" service improvement for the year, and a poster presentation to the chief information officer.

Note: This person even provided a graph that showed the 76 percent reduction in completion time.

As you read these examples, what did you think or feel? Did they seem bragging, arrogant, selfish, egotistical, or chest-thumping? Of course not, they were factual reports of organizational impacts, concisely delivered. Even if you were not part of this industry or company, you had a very clear idea of what the problem was, what action the person or team took, and the result or impact to the organization, which was impressive. Effective leaders are able to communicate their value and to demonstrate their team's value to the larger whole. The key to helping your Inner Leader emerge is to change your paradigm about communicating your impact and that of your team. Hence, once you learn to communicate your successes in this manner, more people will begin to understand the exact impact that you make, and your Inner Leader will be smiling.

CASE STUDY

When Edward came to me, he had just started another new job. We discussed his strengths and it turns out that Edward was a very outgoing and positive person. He got excited about everything and he was excited about this new opportunity. He was also a man of action, so he had already accomplished two big tasks in the first month on the job. The new job was to build a team for a new venture that the company was pursuing.

So far, all good stuff. But, Edward's first problem, as he defined it to me, was "Vickie, when I go in to talk with my boss, I get all excited and then she gives me one-word answers … It is so frustrating, What should I do?" Edward and I developed a communication strategy to use with his boss that was clear, concise, and very much to the point.

In his next meeting, he described his first two accomplishments to her using the CAR format, where each story was only five sentences. Although it felt a little unnatural to him, he found that his boss actually answered him and asked a few questions. Edward felt the success!

WHAT IS YOUR CAREER CURRENCY?

The result of communicating your impact concisely and precisely is that your listener gains clarity. The other benefit of this technique is that your CAR stories become your *career currency*. It is a fact that you have accomplished these successes, and no one can take that away from you. These accomplishments are therefore your career currency to use as you move forward in your career journey. To let your Inner Leader emerge, you have to know, understand, and be able to communicate your successes succinctly. The CAR format is a perfect technique by which to do that.

Let's explore this concept of career currency a bit more. Are you cheating yourself out of correctly reflecting your career currency? The story that I like to tell is that I can go into any company, in any industry, in any function, and at any level and ask a person to show me his or her most recent performance review. In my experience, 90 percent of the time that performance review will document status and activities, not impact. For example, the performance review will have such information as worked with X customer to improve relations (activity), successfully completed ABC project (status), cut budget and managed four subordinates (activity). If your performance review sounds like this, you are doing yourself a disservice by not representing the impact of your activities. As a leader, you need to be attuned at all times to your impact on your organization. I remember a time when Michael Dell, president and founder of Dell computers, had constant streaming of Dell's stock price and number of units sold. At that time, those were his two most important impacts to his company, and he was constantly aware, to the point where he used to start many of his presentations by quoting those two statistics. For some of us, that is a bit extreme, but the message is still the same. Michael Dell was constantly aware of his team's impact on the company.

Below is the gold nugget of this chapter. If you can discipline yourself and your team to do Impact Exercise 2, you will see a huge difference in how you are perceived in your organization. Your Inner Leader will emerge and will become very visible.

IMPACT EXERCISE 2: USE CAR STORIES AS A RECORD OF CAREER CURRENCY

Discipline yourself to write three CAR stories about your accomplishments each month. That is, at most, 15 sentences (five sentences per CAR statement). At the end of the year, you will have 36 powerful impact statements as a record of your career currency. Imagine how easy it will be to provide input for your annual performance review. No more stressing at the end of the year to come up with accomplishments.

By having 36 data points, you will probably begin to see a trend in exactly what types of results you bring in time over time. This can be very helpful during an end-of-the-year review that turns into a development talk. Having data points that prove you are a master at X will then drive the conversation to ask the question "Do I want to continue to do more of X, or am I looking to become a master at Y?"

Even better, for those of you who have direct reports, request that they write three CAR stories per month. Initially this might take some learning on their part and some teaching on your part, but after a few months they will become quite good at writing concise CAR stories with documented and detailed (numbered) results. Although this will make it easy for them to provide year-end information, it is also a fabulous way for you as their manager to stay in touch with what they are accomplishing. It leaves this data trail of what mastery the individuals on your team are developing. Also, let us not forget the sports analogy of the team concept: Their impact becomes your impact.

To make this perfectly clear, a team member's CAR statement would read:

> Uncovered _____ challenge and took _____
> action, and the result was _____.

The team lead's CAR statement would read:

> Led the team that uncovered _____ challenge and
> took _____ action, and the result was _____.

Can you see how this idea of writing three CAR stories a month can have a huge effect on how your team communicates its impact?

This exercise is the gold nugget of the chapter because if you and your team simply make this one change, the results will be staggering, and the impact of your Inner Leader will become visible.

CAR STORIES FOR CAREER LEADERSHIP AND SUCCESS

Just as we have seen in the previous chapters, there are many uses for your strengths and values. Once you have written your past 20 CAR stories and you are keeping a running list of three CAR stories a month, there are several places where you can use and communicate these examples of career currency. The specific uses to examine in the rest of this chapter are using CAR stories in performance reviews and when you introduce yourself.

CAR Stories in Performance Reviews

Although this was stated before, I wanted to give you a real-world example of how a person shifted his thinking about using CAR stories for his performance review.

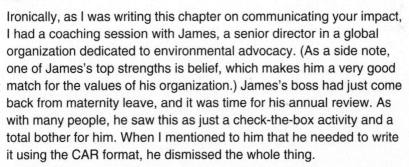

Ironically, as I was writing this chapter on communicating your impact, I had a coaching session with James, a senior director in a global organization dedicated to environmental advocacy. (As a side note, one of James's top strengths is belief, which makes him a very good match for the values of his organization.) James's boss had just come back from maternity leave, and it was time for his annual review. As with many people, he saw this as just a check-the-box activity and a total bother for him. When I mentioned to him that he needed to write it using the CAR format, he dismissed the whole thing.

As his coach, it was my job to press the point to him. James not only needed to write up his CAR statements for the past year (which he had not faithfully done) but also needed to prepare actively for his review. Because his boss had not been involved for four months, he needed to impress on her the impact that he and his team had created while she was gone. I reminded him that part of his value was continuing the team's impact while his boss was away—after all, she is still part of the team and has some ownership in James's impact as well. Although he initially made a face, his intellect took over, and he realized that this would be a win-win for both of them. James told me later that it was the best annual review that he'd ever had.

Whatever format your organization uses for performance reviews, your CAR stories will be the foundation. Many times organizations will ask you to match your accomplishments with a list of leadership competencies or attributes that the company sees as necessary for a leader to demonstrate mastery. For my clients, it is then easy to take their CAR story and match it to the list of attributes that their company requires. You will be amazed at how robust your annual review documentation will be when you have 36 five-sentence CAR stories to use as the foundation of telling your performance story. Also, from a real-world perspective, if your peers do not fully buy into the CAR format, your using it in your review will simply blow away any comparison with others; because your review with written CAR stories will be exponentially more robust.

In future chapters we will talk more about promoting yourself, your accomplishments, and your personal brand. And here I feel the need to give a small caveat to you, the reader. Are you thinking that this could backfire on you, that a boss would begin to take your CAR stories and not give you credit? The way to ensure that you get credit is to spread your stories around actively. You want to tell everyone with whom you come in contact your impact and successes. Although a certain finesse needs to accompany the communication of these stories, the result is the same. Many people with whom you work will begin to understand the impact of what you do.

CAR Stories in Your Personal Introduction

In terms of introductions—I have a dream. In this dream businesspeople introduce themselves talking about their *what* and *who*. As we have seen in previous chapters, your *who* is your strengths and values. Your *what* is your impact communicated through CAR stories.

Imagine introducing yourself at the kickoff meeting of a project. Instead of saying, "My name is _____ and I am in the _____ department," suppose you said what your strength is, gave an example of it in the form of a CAR story, and then closed by saying what you believe that you can contribute to the team.

I know that right now you might be thinking how ridiculous that would be. So let me give you another example. Suppose that you are in the elevator at work and the *big dog* gets in with you. The big dog can be the chief executive officer (CEO) or any C-level person, your boss's boss, an important customer or stakeholder, or someone important to your world. What do you say? Do you want to say something that is memorable, or do you want to shrink into the corner? Because you are stuck there for at least the next 10 seconds, it would be good if you had something prepared to say. The other example is if you know that you are going to meet the big dog, how do you prepare, and what do you say? Hopefully the next two stories will help convince you to use this format.

Penelope was in a dead-end job. Because she was very outgoing and a great presenter, she volunteered at the local hospital once a month to go out into the community and give presentations about breast and prostate cancer. She had been doing this for the past three years and just loved it. When the coordinator of all the volunteers left to follow her husband's work in another state, the position became open. Because she was a known quantity, she got the job. Penelope excelled at this job.

About eight months into her job, she was going to be at a big benefit with the CEO of the hospital. She called me, concerned about what she was going to talk about with him. After a few minutes of casual conversation, I asked her to define what her biggest success had been in the first eight months of her job—that was easy when she was just talking with me. Together we crafted the following statement:

> Hello Mr. CEO, I am Penelope and I am the coordinator of all of the hospital's 300 volunteers who go out into the community to speak on our behalf. I am especially

passionate about breast and prostate cancer and have turned that passion into the following achievement. Since I started at the hospital eight months ago, I have increased our volunteer team by 29 percent and decreased our budget by 16 percent. Next year I intend to double that.

Imagine the CEO's remarks; he was thrilled to hear this and spent the next 10 minutes asking Penelope the details of how she had accomplished this. Penelope's Inner Leader was smiling.

Now that you have heard Penelope's story, it is easy for her to shorten this for the 10-second elevator speech, for the introduction at a new project team meeting, or for that all-important customer meeting. The shortened version might look like this:

I am Penelope and I coordinate 300 volunteers who speak within the community. My passion is breast and prostate cancer, and I have turned that into the following achievement. In the past 8 months, I have increased our volunteer team by 29 percent and decreased our budget by 16 percent. Next year I intend to double that.

Practicing what you will say when introducing yourself is a necessity. Remember, it is simply precisely and concisely communicating the facts about you. This is so important for your Inner Leader to emerge that I feel the need to communicate another story.

I was working with Claudia through the Duke Leadership Program. She worked in North Carolina, for a global biotherapeutic company headquartered in France. She was the vice president reporting to the chief information officer (CIO) and had told me that for her next job she wanted to be the CIO of a medium-sized company within the next three years.

She had been leading the company's Systems Applications and Products (SAP) implementation projects, first in America and then in France, whose implementation she had just completed. She came to our call ecstatic that both implementations had gone well and that she would finally get to meet the CEO in France next week. When I asked her what she was planning on saying to him, she stopped cold. So we began to brainstorm and I asked her what it was that she attributed her super success to. Although she told me that very easily, I explained to her that she needed to tell the CEO the same thing. Now her nerves and excuses began to surface. This is what we practiced and what she ultimately said to the CEO:

> Monsieur _____, it is a pleasure to finally meet you, especially on this occasion when we are celebrating the success of the SAP implementation. I would like to share with you that I have a philosophy that I deployed throughout the implementation. That philosophy is to hire people who are smarter than I am, and then let them work their magic. Certainly I coordinated all of the global efforts, as being the conductor of a team is one of my strengths and I enjoyed watching my team do their best. Also, our SAP representative has told me that America and France were in the top 10 percent of successful implementations that they had this year.

What did you think of these two introduction scenarios? Could you introduce yourself like this? Would you feel comfortable doing it? Do you want to try to build your introduction, but so-called real work always gets in the way? What could motivate you, or who can you find to motivate you to get busy and prepare your introduction? The next time you find yourself in a situation where you need to introduce yourself, you will be happy that you had prepared and your Inner Leader will burst forth.

On a personal note, whenever I give presentations or workshops I always introduce myself by telling and describing my three strengths and then a CAR. My introduction sounds like this:

I am honored to be here today to talk about _____.
I come to you with three strengths; they are:

1. Positivity: I am the glass half-full person.

2. Partnership: My only definition of success is the success of my clients.

3. I am a maximizer, which means that I excel and get my energy from working with good people and helping to make them great.

That is why I am thrilled to be here with you today, because you are my perfect audience and it is my job in the next two hours to give you five techniques that you can deploy to move yourself from good to great.

Then I add in a CAR relevant to the topic. How does that sound to you? Hopefully it sounds quite natural because it always comes off well.

I will let you in on a little secret: The first time that I stood up in front of an audience and said that I was a maximizer, I would rather have cut off my right arm; I was that scared. And what made me so scared? The answer is that little voice of doubt in each of our heads. My little voice kept a running negative stream of thoughts that I had to work hard to silence. It sounded like this: "Maximizer, what a stupid word, they are all going to look at me like I have three heads or have lost my mind, why am I doing this anyway, I should have never taken this job and just stayed home today, maximizer who ever came up with that word anyway," and on and on. That negative voice in our heads is a huge obstacle to overcome when making the choice to introduce yourself by communicating your *what* and your *who*. There is no magic here but to become aware that it will exist. Next you need to learn to accept the fact that you have the choice to let that voice take over or not to listen to it. The success that you will begin to realize by learning to communicate in this manner will be the best antidote to that negative voice inside of your head.

The formula for building your introduction is:

- What is your name and function?

- What are your greatest strengths?

- How do you use your strengths?
- What is a most recent impact of using your strength (CAR story)?
- What does that mean (benefit) to your audience?

What was said at the beginning of this chapter? The statement was that the concept of developing and using your CAR stories is challenging. And you might have a little voice inside your head right now giving you that running negative commentary or potentially giving you every excuse in the book of why this might be fine for others, but you can't do it because of _____. Turn off that bad radio station in your head; let's get on with it and unleash your Inner Leader. You have done hard things in your life before and have reaped the rewards. So come on; get to work building and using your CAR stories.

CASE STUDY

Edward was having much more success communicating with his boss by using CAR stories. Then the most amazing thing happened. Three weeks after the first meeting when he communicated his CAR stories, he and his boss were in a larger meeting of his boss's boss and all their reports. When his boss was called on to discuss her team, she used Edward's CAR statement almost verbatim, giving him the credit for such an early win for the new team. Edward was thrilled; not only was his Inner Leader emerging, but he was also leading up.

This propelled him to talk with his boss about his strengths and where he believed that he could make the most impact in the creation of this new team. His boss was very open to his suggestions, and now Edward is one of the rare few in his company who has a job where he uses his strengths about 80 percent of the time and faithfully writes his three CAR stories a month, which he then appropriately communicates. Edward has identified his next promotion and is making a point of communicating his impact to those who can make that promotion happen. His Inner Leader is confidently moving forward.

IMPACT CHAPTER SUMMARY

- Communicating your accomplishments in the CAR (Challenge, Action, Result) format is the technique that successful leaders use to demonstrate their impact.

- Your CAR stories are your career currency, or the foundation upon which you build your career.

CAR stories can be successfully used in performance reviews and introductions to concisely communicate your impact to the organization. You can also match your CAR stories to company leadership competencies when writing performance reviews.

- Impact Exercise 1: Write 20 CAR stories for your past successes, and then edit them down to a maximum of five sentences per CAR story. The result must have a number in it.

- Impact Exercise 2: Discipline yourself and your team to write three CAR stories per month. Each year you will then contribute 36 CAR stories to your career currency.

- Successful leaders are adept at easily communicating their impact and the impact of their team to anyone, anytime, anywhere.

CHAPTER 5

Personal Brand: How Do Others See You?

ersonal branding is your unique promise of value. It is composed of your strengths, values, target audience, results, and benefits. Building and using your personal brand is not a check-the-box activity; it is a lifelong commitment to precisely and concisely telling the facts about you, on a daily basis. Doing it often will make it a natural part of you, in other words, a habit. Perceptions about you are constantly being reinforced by your audience. If they are good, keep them; if they are incorrect, you must work hard to change them. You are 100 percent in control of your personal brand. Your personal brand allows you to put your mark on everything that you do.

Meet Chin, an auditor by education with experience working for one of the top four accounting firms in Los Angeles. He has been a partner in the firm for seven years. The firm selected a few key partners to go through a personal branding training program, and I was the coach who was going to help Chin through this program. When I first met him, he was excited to have been chosen for this elite group but had no idea what personal branding was or what it could do to help him. He had heard the buzzwords and intellectually understood the concept of branding in general, especially as it relates to large companies having a brand, but was cautious, confused, and a bit distrustful of the whole personal branding process. It was going to be an interesting engagement for me.

WHAT IS A PERSONAL BRAND?

When the subject of personal branding is discussed, do you have the same cautious and confused reaction that Chin did? Let's start this chapter by discussing what personal branding is and how it can benefit you.

Whenever I talk with business professionals about personal branding, I bring along some props. (See Figure 5.1.)

Figure 5.1 Which One Would You Buy?

When I take out these two cans, I ask people which one they would want to buy. Unless you are super adventurous, like to be surprised, or love everything that has ever come out of a can, you will probably pick the can with the label on it. Why? Because you know what the product is made up of. The outside packaging gives you information about what you are buying.

I then bring out the following two cans (Figure 5.2) and ask, "Which one would you like to buy?"

Now the decision is more intricate. Both products are similar and your mind now has to go through some sort of thought process in terms of what product you want to buy.

How can the example of these cans help us in promoting ourselves and making better business decisions? Suppose we want to hire a project manager. Now imagine that the cans in Figure 5.1 were two project managers, and you were going to buy, so to speak, one of them to run your project. It is a no-brainer; you pick the one with more information, as long as that information is a fit for you. The point is that in today's world when buying a product, the more information you have about that product, the more informed decision you can make.

Figure 5.2 With More Information, Which One Would You Buy?

In Figure 5.1, if you were looking for a tomato soup project manager, you would not buy a chicken noodle project manager, and the other can does not tell you what flavor project manager it is.

Now let's look at Figure 5.2. If you wanted to buy a chicken noodle project manager, from the outward appearance, they are both the project manager that you wanted, but they have subtle differences. From the front of the can, you can begin to see the differences, but of course, you probably want more information before you make your purchase decision. Think about your work world now; are all people with the same title the same? Do they approach problems the same way? Do they build relationships the same way? Do they drive results the same way? Of course not, each person is different. These cans serve as an analogy to provide more complete information about ourselves every day so that those around us are very sure of what is inside of us and what we will bring to the work place.

Now let's look at Figure 5.3. On the back of the soup cans, we begin to get much more detail about the contents or character of these products. For example, one needs to have water added; the amount

Figure 5.3 Now with Much More Information, Which One Would You Buy?

or servings that you get are slightly different; the amount of protein, sodium, and carbohydrates are different. That then gives more information upon which to make a decision.

An extension of the information on the can is the external marketing for each of these products. This external marketing is creating a perception of the product, and more important it creates a promise to the person who buys it and uses it. For Campbell's, the soup promises to be good. For Progresso, the soup promises to help you lose weight and to be tasty.

With this information, we can now make a very informed decision about what soup we want to buy because the back of the label has lots of information about the product, and we know its value because of the external marketing.

Let's now take this analogy back to choosing a project manager for a new project. Although we have two project manager candidates, they need to provide more information so that we can make a more informed choice. That information could be very factual, such as their experience, education, and types of projects worked on in the past (in terms of number, size, and scope). Similar to the protein, sodium, and carbohydrates content on the soup cans, there is also the value part of the equation. What is each project manager's perceived value? What is his or her external reputation? Does each manager drive results by using gantt charts, program evaluation review technique (PERT) charts, and work breakdown structures (WBS)? If that is the type of project manager that you want, then "buy" him or her. If the project manager drives results by building relationships with his or her team and stakeholders, and if this is what you need to get this project to closure, then "buy" him or her. It is important to match your employees' strengths and values to a project and not just match their numbers. If we really needed the relationship project manager and we "bought" the analytical project manager, it would be disastrous for both sides.

I like this analogy because so many people have a negative reaction to the concept of personal branding. They think of the person who is a braggadocios or a chest thumper. That is not what personal branding is.

Personal branding is concisely and precisely communicating the facts about you to your target audience so that they can make an informed decision about working with you.

I hope that the simple analogy of the soup cans will keep you focused throughout this chapter on what the goal of personal branding is.

PERSONAL BRANDING IS ABOUT HOW OTHERS PERCEIVE YOU

Personal branding is an ongoing piece of your daily and weekly routine, just as much as brushing your teeth or checking e-mail each day is. It is about deciding who you are, what you do, and how to communicate that on an ongoing basis to the people next to you and across the globe.

It is all about how others perceive you. Within 30 seconds of meeting you, people judge your:

- Economic level
- Educational level
- Social position
- Level of sophistication
- Level of success

Within 4 minutes of meeting you, people judge your:

- Trustworthiness
- Reliability
- Intelligence
- Capability
- Friendliness
- Confidence

Wow, those are some amazing statistics that totally support the idea that you never get a second chance to make a first impression. The interesting piece of this is that people will continue to reinforce within themselves their first impression of you. For example, let's say that when Maria met Sam, he was having a bad day. He was not prepared for the meeting, was very sloppy in his presentation, and gave the impression that he just did not care. No matter how many more times Maria interacts with Sam, and even if for the next 10 interactions, his performance is stellar, the next time that he messes up, Maria is going to use that time and that time only to reinforce her perception that Sam is not engaged. Therefore, not only is it important to make the correct first impression, but also if you make the wrong impression, it takes a monumental effort to change that person's perception of you. Think back; have you ever had an incorrect perception about someone? What happened to make you change that perception? We are, by nature, human beings who believe that we are always right. Have you ever gotten off on the wrong foot with a new boss or new customer? How much harder did that make your working relationship until you got things back on the right track?

Below is my biggest tenet about personal branding:

> *Perceptions about you are constantly being reinforced by your audience. If they are good, keep them; if they are incorrect, you must work hard to change them.*
> *You are 100 percent in control of your personal brand.*

This is a hard concept to swallow. My typical pushback on this statement is "I cannot control what others think of me. Vickie, this is a little over the top." We are not talking about changing your behavior to impress your boss or the very important person who comes into town for two days. We are talking about communicating a fixed piece of who you are and what you value. If your mind-set is that you do not care what others think, then you are only shortchanging yourself and potentially even sabotaging yourself. If you are a great-performing chicken noodle soup employee, what is the problem with showing that, rather than being the label-less can of soup?

Are you ready to change your paradigm? Remember that the first two steps of the Change Model are Awareness and Acceptance. You are becoming aware by simply reading this chapter and thinking about personal branding. Then if you accept this awareness and make the commitment to show up consistently demonstrating the perceptions that you want people to have of you, eventually, you will change people's perceptions of you, until they have the perception that you want. Is this a tall order? Yes. Is this easy? No. Will you reap major rewards by building and using your personal brand? Absolutely.

ARE YOU ON THE CAREER LEDGE?

Personal branding is about who you are; it is about showing your authentic self. A personal brand shows the world who you are, what you stand for, and what results you can deliver. There are times when I begin working with business professionals that they become aware of the fact that they have somehow drifted away from their core foundation. Somehow over the years they have lost their authentic self. There are stories of people leaving their soul outside as they enter the doors of their workplace. Others tell of changing themselves so much to work with a boss, a certain customer set, or a company that they hardly recognize themselves anymore. When I start talking about personal branding, I like to ask, "How is it possible that we sometimes get so far away from our core or foundation in our jobs?" I then tell the "Are you on the ledge?" story.

We never plan or intend to get on the ledge—it just happens. Here is a running commentary on how it happens.

You are born. You learn to walk and talk. You go to elementary school. You learn to read and write. You go to high school; you learn algebra and history. Then you have to decide where you will go to

Figure 5.4 Are You on the Career Ledge?

work or where you will go to college. Sometimes the college decision is based on anyone who will take me, anyone who will give me money, anyplace far away from home, or wherever my girlfriend or boyfriend at the time is going. Then you get to college and you learn lots of new things; some of them are actually useful. You take classes in new subjects and explore new areas of interest. Then you have to decide on a major. Sometimes the decision is based on any major where I do not have to take an 8 AM class, any major that has pass/fail classes, or any major where I am guaranteed to get a job, or you might actually decide on a major of a subject that you like and are good at.

Take a breath.

Then you have to get your first job. Your decision is based on anyone who will hire me, a job in a location where living costs are less expensive, a job in a company whose values I admire, or the job that pays the most. So you go along and you do your job, you get new jobs, and you get promotions. One day your boss comes to you and asks you to spend the weekend doing next year's department budget on a spreadsheet a mile long, because he has been called in on an important project. What do you do? Of course, you change all your weekend plans and you do the budget—and you do a good job. So what happens next year at budget time? You did such a good job the year before that the boss gives you the job of doing the budget again. After a few years of doing the budget (which you hate and does not use any of your strengths), you do such a good job that your boss finally offers you a promotion as the department's financial person.

You wake up one morning hating to go to work because you used to do creative marketing creative work, and now you are stuck in your cubicle doing spreadsheets all day. You realize that you are on the career ledge. What do you do?

Initially when you hear this story, it might seem very reactionary, or it might seem like this person does not have much selectivity in him or her. You might see this on the surface, yet many clients have come to me lost because they have made decisions along the way that have taken them away from their core. If you resonate with this story, or you know someone who has faced this type of challenge, it is time to pull back to your core and really think about *who* you are and *what* you do.

I have had countless clients come to me, and we have discovered that they are on the career ledge. No matter the industry, their function, their level, or their personal circumstances, they have found themselves on the ledge. My heart hurts for them, because it is not easy to take yourself off the career ledge—it does not happen in one day, and it is not a check-the-box activity. But, and this is a big but—if you start at the beginning and you make the time, you can discover the truth about *who* you are and *what* you do.

There is a second part to this story. When you are on the career ledge, you keep hoping that you can *find yourself again*, when you walk through the company's doors at night and go home to your *real life*. This is the lie that we sometimes tell ourselves, that *I will find myself again as I leave this place tonight*. If you are on the career ledge, this chapter will be critically important for you.

A note here: Discovering who you are and what you do was covered in depth in Chapters 2 and 3, respectively. If you have not read those chapters or done the exercises, I suggest that you go back and review those concepts.

In this chapter, I will give you five steps to developing your personal brand. For the purposes of this book and discovering your Inner Leader, my five steps will give you a personal brand to be proud of to help get you where you need to go to unleash the leader within you.

Meet Philip, an attorney with a national cellular tower company. He led a group of 12 paralegals, and his team worked on more than 10,000 contractual documents a year. As our coaching engagement unfolded, one of the things that Philip told me was that his boss was always telling him that to be promoted, he had to be more strategic. When I asked Philip what his boss meant by this, he simply shook his head in pure ignorance. Although we tried a few coaching techniques and exercises, one exercise finally shed some light on the issue. I had asked Philip to observe the behavior of his boss and his boss's peers for signs of what they value.

In our next meeting, Philip reported that he had the answer: His boss and his peers were all *process* driven and Philip was *results* driven. This was a huge moment of awareness for Philip. By way of confirming his discovery, he related the following story.

There had been an issue and Philip had resolved it. The next thing he knew, the corporate attorneys were in his office along with his boss. At the end of the meeting, the boss sided with the corporate attorney, even though the issue had been resolved. Philip was not feeling support from his boss until he realized that his boss valued *process over results*.

This is a story that illustrates a person who found himself on the career ledge. Somehow Philip had gotten himself in an organization where his strengths and values were not a match for what the organization wanted of him. Philip accepted this fact and decided to move to an organization that was a better match. Prepared with his knowledge of *who* he is and *what* accomplishments he produces, it ended up that Philip's drive toward executing results was so very strong that he was able to use that as the basis for his personal brand.

Armed with this knowledge, he left his company and built a whole career transition plan around the fact that he was the results guy. He quickly got a job at a start-up that basically had no processes and became a major share owner in this company five years ago. Philip was 100 percent in control of others' perceptions of him, and once he found the environment that valued his uniqueness, he was happy and productive. Philip's Inner Leader was unleashed. In the next section we will examine the five steps towards building a personal brand.

FIVE STEPS TOWARD PERSONAL BRANDING

The first three steps are about knowing yourself:

Step 1 *Who* are you?
- What unique strengths do you have?

Step 2 *What* do you do?
- What have you accomplished in your career (Challenge, Action, Result [CAR] stories)?

Step 3 What is your unique promise of value?
- What is your unique value?

The next two steps are about using your personal brand to maximize performance:

Step 4 How do you leverage your personal brand?
- How do you communicate your personal brand?

Step 5 What does a successful brand look like?
- How do you know that you have successfully lived your personal brand?

Did you notice that the first two steps have already been discussed? If you have been reading and diligently doing the exercises, you are already aware of your strengths and your impact. If you have skipped to this chapter, then you might want to at least skim Chapters 2 and 4, to get the gist of what the first two steps are.

In step 3, I use the phrase *your unique promise of value*. I believe that this is the essence of what a personal brand is: that before you even show up on the scene, your unique promise of value precedes you. Just as Philip learned, his unique promise of value is that it is guaranteed that he will drive results in your company. The word *promise* here is important. When you make a promise, it is personal. It is you making that personal guarantee that you will provide this level and type of values. Many other personal branding concepts will talk about a value exchange or your value statement. I encourage you to embrace the idea that your personal brand is a promise to your listener: It is a promise of the value that you bring to them.

Below is my template for building your personal brand:

I use my (strengths) _____1_____ to do (what)
_____2_____ to whom (target audience) _____3_____
so that the target audience does (what) _____4_____ and
gets (what results) _____5_____.

Let's take each piece of this puzzle. In Chapter 2 you have already identified your *who* (strengths), and in Chapter 4 you have already identified what actions you take to drive your *what* (results); here you get to marry the two.

A word of caution here: Some of you might be tempted to fill in the template before going through the exercises below. If you do that, then

I suggest that you do that, then do the exercises that follow, and then compare your refined personal brand statement to your initial filled-in template. Take your confidence temperature, so to speak, when you have looked at both. How frequently will you use the statement that you just took a swing at versus the one that you have taken the time to think about? Do the exercises, take your temperature again, and even do it a third time. There should be an incremental increase in confidence and authenticity once you have really dug in and built your statement from the ground up. Your statement will then become an authentic part of you.

PERSONAL BRAND EXERCISE 1: WHO ARE YOU?

I use my (strengths) _____1_____ to do (what)
_____2_____ to whom (target audience) _____3_____
so that the target audience does (what) _____4_____ and
gets (what results) _____5_____.

Look at your list of strengths that you built in Chapter 2, and pick, at most, the two strengths that you seem to use most often. One way of doing this is to look at your list of 20 CAR stories that you built in Chapter 4 and for each success, name the strength that you used to get this result. When you go back and review your list, there should be one or two strengths that you seem to pull on the most. You should use these two to fill in the first blank in your personal brand statement. In this step you are looking for your strengths. For Philip, this was easy; his top strength was driving results.

PERSONAL BRAND EXERCISE 2: WHAT DO YOU DO?

I use my (strengths) _____1_____ to do (what)
_____2_____ to whom (target audience) _____3_____
so that the target audience does (what) _____4_____ and
gets (what results) _____5_____.

Review your list of CAR stories that you built in Chapter 4, and pay particular attention to the action step of your success story. Ask yourself what one or two actions you seem to take consistently to produce your results. For example, in the action that you take, do you inspire, activate, analyze, report, train, coordinate, clarify, launch, negotiate, influence, mentor, partner, build, strategize, develop, or upgrade? You will want to use these words in this exercise. In this exercise you are looking to get to the next level of how you use your strengths.

Review your list of CAR statements and ask yourself this question: What is the one result that you seem to have more than anything else? Is it that you reduce costs, improve processes, make more sales than anyone else, always deliver early and under budget, improve efficiency or productivity, deliver more and better training than anyone else, reduce and mitigate risks, keep employees and customers happy, or lead your team to do any of the above by coaching, directing, demanding, or analyzing? Fill in blank 2 with your answer.

As an example, Philip had a passion for not allowing contractual details to slow down the process of making money for the company. So the first two parts of his personal brand read, "I use my assertive nature to drive results, which ensures that all revenues can be collected on time and can keep the company's bottom line positive."

PERSONAL BRAND EXERCISE 3: WHAT IS YOUR UNIQUE PROMISE OF VALUE?

I use my (strengths) _____1_____ to do (what)
_____2_____ to whom (target audience) _____3_____
so that the target audience does (what) _____4_____ and
gets (what results) _____5_____.

Although your target audience has not been specifically discussed, if you look at your list of 20 or more CAR statements, you will most likely find your target audience in those statements. Your target audience can be found in the challenge or your results. For example, your target audience could be internal or external customers, internal or external suppliers, internal or external stakeholders, or your specific group that you work in. Sort through your CAR stories and see what the patterns are in terms of who your target audience is. Add that in blank 3.

To further clarify, you do not need different statements for different target audiences. Typically I find that people gravitate to a specific target audience whether it is because of their characteristic or because of their job function. For example, I gravitate toward already successful business professionals who want to get to the next level or to the top of their game. That is my target audience. Philip's target audience was every contracting company that his firm did business with. Chin's target audience was companies in Korea, China, and Japan who want to do business in the United States.

PERSONAL BRAND EXERCISE 4: WHAT ARE YOUR RESULTS?

> I use my (strengths) _____1_____ to do (what) _____2_____ to whom (target audience) _____3_____ so that the target audience does (what) _____4_____ and gets (what results) _____5_____.

Blanks 4 and 5 might be a bit more difficult to fill in, but I believe that you do have the answers also in your CAR statements. The way to uncover these answers is to take out a piece of paper and make two vertical columns on the page. Label one of the columns *results* and the second column *benefits*. Then to fill in blank 4, look at each result statement in each CAR, and find the result. Some examples of results are if you:

- Consistently reduce costs for your external customers
- Consistently deliver and launch new products (projects, marketing materials, or legal advice) that make money in the short term
- Consistently deliver training to your target audience (salespeople, call center, or business units); your results are the amount of training delivered and the grades given to you on your feedback forms (for example, "Over a six-month period training feedback averaged 4.87 on a 5-point scale.")

Once you have made your list of results, move on to the last blank to complete your personal branding statement using the formula above.

PERSONAL BRAND EXERCISE 5: WHAT ARE THE BENEFITS OF YOUR RESULTS?

> I use my (strengths) _____1_____ to do (what)
> _____2_____ to whom (target audience) _____3_____
> so that the target audience does (what) _____4_____ and
> gets (what results) _____5_____.

You are now ready to fill in blank 5. Go back to the columns that you made above and look at the benefit side. You now want to fill in blank 5 with the benefit statement. Some examples of benefits are if you:

- Consistently reduce costs for your external customers, then the benefit is that year over year you directly contribute to the bottom line of your customers by an average of X percent.

- Consistently deliver and launch new products (projects, marketing, materials, or legal advice) that make money in the short term, then the benefit is improving the projected launch results by X percent.

- Consistently deliver training to your target audience (salespeople, call center, or business units), and your results are the amount of training delivered and the grades given to you on your feedback forms (for example, "Over a six-month period training feedback averaged 4.87 on a 5-point scale."), then the benefit is that the sales team of 20,000 people deployed globally saved 5 hours per week by learning how to use the automated time sheet application on their iPads.

Once you have discovered the benefits that your results have provided to your target audience, you are ready to complete your personal branding statement.

It is always helpful to have real-life examples. More information is in the chapter case study and a list of personal branding statements below. Although some of these might sound long to you, the written statements are for your written marketing collateral.

When speaking your personal brand statement, I suggest that you think more in terms of talking points or bullet points. This then allows you to insert them in a conversation with words around the talking points that will make the conversation flow more easily. Go ahead; try it and see what you can build to concisely and precisely communicate your authentic and unique promise of value.

EXAMPLES: PERSONAL BRAND STATEMENTS

CASE STUDY

Chin had a harder time than Philip with developing his personal branding statement. Yet the more that we talked and the more he thought about how he wanted to influence the perceptions of his peers, bosses, staff, stakeholders, and external clients, he became more committed to this than ever. He steadily did all the exercises and then some. One extra thing that he did was find three close colleagues to whom, when he got confused or frustrated, he would go for confirmation. Through this process Chin and I discovered some interesting things about him. One, he was a citizen of the world. He was born in Korea, lived in China and Japan (and spoke the associated languages), and had been in Los Angeles for the past eight years. Two, he had found a niche in his firm where his goal was to help companies bring their business to the United States (help with international transfer pricing and taxation). Three, he was courageous. There was never a situation that arose that he did not rise to the occasion to try to help his clients. Four, he loved to network. He discovered that whatever issues his clients brought to him, give him 24 hours and he could find *someone* to help them. *Wow,* would you like to buy that can of soup?

Now, it took Chin about six months to feel truly comfortable with all these characteristics. Did he get frustrated? Yes. As a matter of fact, I remember more than once when he would stop everything, look at me, and say, "But Vickie, I am just an auditor." That is when I would request that he talk with his three colleagues and ask them whether he was just an auditor.

Finally we developed Chin's talking points and personal brand statement, and I share it with you below. First we developed his personal brand talking points from previous chapters input, which are:

- Huge international network
- Citizen of the world
- International financial prowess
- Build Japanese, Korean, Chinese business in the US.
- Courageous and pioneering spirit

Then we built his personal brand statement using the formula presented in this chapter:

As a trusted advisor with a global vision, I am revered by my clients, not only for my international financial prowess but also for my pioneering spirit of tapping into my seemingly limitless network and converging the best authorities to be the cross-cultural facilitator to bring Japanese, Korean, and Chinese clients' business to the United States.

How awesome is that? Once he got comfortable with that statement, my maximizer took over and I asked him to build a follow-on statement that was less formal and more verbally expressive. Here it is:

I do this as a natural networker who can connect you with the right *people, with the* right *methods, with the* right *resources to make your business in the United States soar!*

Would you like to do business with that can of soup? Absolutely, and Chin's Client portfolio has increased by 30 percent in just two short years!

Here are more examples of personal brand statements:

Personal Brand Statement Example One:

My niche is as the technology guru in the rheumatology field. I get inspired by what new technology can do to access cutting-edge data and create resources for the team. I am known for using iPad apps and compiling conference abstracts/talks to be accessed at the touch of a button. The combination of biotech and information technology is the key to improving patient treatment outcomes and is what I impact.

Talking Points:

- Technology guru
- Inspired by new technology
- Information access at the touch of a button
- Combination of biotech and infotech is the key to improving patient treatment options.

Personal Brand Statement Example Two:

I am a champion for patients of all socio-economic backgrounds to get access to the medical treatments that they need. I do this in two ways. One is by impacting clinical trials to include more underserved populations. And two by passionately educating physicians and healthcare providers to use more cutting-edge data to reduce morbidity and mortality.

Talking Points:

- Champion for underserved populations
- Get them into clinical trials
- Educate their providers
- Reduce morbidity and mortality

Personal Brand Statement Example Three:

I am the glue that holds disparate pieces of the project together. I am known for doing whatever it takes to get the job done. I have a track record in highly visible projects, of successful product launches that are delivered on time, within budget, with a happy team and that exceed financial metrics to positively impact the company's bottom line.

Talking Points

- Glue that holds project together
- I do whatever it takes
- History of successful product launches
- Deliver on time, within budget and with a happy team
- Committed to exceeding financial metrics

Personal Brand Statement Example Four:

I combine my strategic futuristic thinking with the unique ability to simplify esoteric concepts; to create innovative and executable approaches for biotech organizations, so that both the company and the patient *win*.

Talking Points

- Strategic thinking
- Simplify esoteric concepts
- Create new approaches
- Company and patients *win*

Personal Brand Statement Example Five:

I have been called a wave of positive energy that builds compassionate relationships of trust and openness to advocate education in the fight against breast cancer to move the death rate to a life rate. Using our assertive nature, commitment to excellence, and in-depth understanding of our customers and the competitive environment, the *xyz* department motivates research and development and marketing executives to design, build, and market innovative products that are at least two steps ahead of competing products.

Talking Points:

- Wave of positive energy
- Move death rate to a life rate
- Leads the *xyz* department to motivate executive's support of innovative prodcuts
- Vision is to stay at least two steps ahead of competing products.

Go ahead; try building your personal brand statement and please do not get discouraged. Follow these steps as your move forward:

1. Refine your statement and talking points until you like it.
2. Make changes from the results of each refinement.

3. Pick a partner who knows you well.

4. Share your refined personal brand statement with your partner and solicit feedback.

5. Adjust and finalize your personal brand statement.

6. Remember your personal brand statement is your unique promise of value.

Start out in a simple mode, and know that you will tweak and modify your personal brand statement as you move forward on your journey to unleashing your Inner Leader.

PUTTING YOUR PERSONAL BRAND TO WORK

Now that you have spent all this time and energy discovering, building, and refining your personal brand statement, it is time to *put your mark on everything you do.*

Figure 5.5 Leave Your Mark on Everything That You Do

It is now time to think about having your personal brand work for you. That means that your personal brand can help you:

- Support the achievement and use of your unique attributes and goals,
- Give your career focus and direction,
- Chart your course of career destination both long and short term,
- Allocate your time and energy,
- Conserve your precious personal resources (time and energy) on irrelevant activities, and
- Create, reach, and review your career goals annually to ensure that you *never* find yourself on the ledge.

Yogi Berra once stated, "If you don't know where you're going, you might end up someplace else." Your personal brand can help act as a decision gate for you. Whenever you are making decisions on the next step in your career, your Inner Leader can take over and use your personal brand statement as a guiding light for career steps. When you look for the next step in your career, make sure that it supports your personal brand.

Personally, I am asked to volunteer for many things and associations. I always use my personal brand as a gate to say yes or no. For example, when I do a pro bono presentation for an association and it is thanking me profusely, I always say, *"Thank you for the opportunity for me to give back to your organization in accordance with my personal brand. I get asked to volunteer lots of my time, and I make it a personal priority to spend my time doing only the activities that I love to do and do well."*

If I am offered a project that I know will not support my personal brand, I will refer it to someone else whose personal brand will support that need and be contented with my decision, knowing that it was the right thing to do. A personal brand is a great gate for time allocation. It also works for work projects.

Another way to make your personal brand work for you is to commit to communicating your personal brand so that all your marketing collateral delivers the same message. Formalize this and build a communications plan for your personal brand. Ask yourself: Who needs to know me (internal and external), and am I reaching them in a meaningful way? Clarifying the people who need to know you is huge. These are the people who can potentially help you reach your goals. These people are also your brand ambassadors, who will reenforce your brand and sing your praises (as long as you give them the music by which they will sing).

You should also think about who the thought leaders in your industry are. Do you know them? Do they know you? How can you leverage them and their thoughts? If you make a conscious decision to monitor your personal brand communication continuously, it will get easier and more fulfilling as time goes on.

PERSONAL BRAND EXERCISE 6: COMMUNICATE YOUR PERSONAL BRAND DAILY

Say your personal brand statement at least once a day. At first this will seem almost impossible but do not despair. Keep looking for times in conversations, meetings, and presentations where you can insert the talking points of your personal brand. What is your goal in doing this? Your goal is that everyone with whom you associate with will begin to understand your unique promise of value. Remember that others' perceptions of you are 100 percent controlled by you. If you say your personal brand statement consistently, within six months, you should begin to hear others describe you in your own words, not theirs. You can then congratulate yourself that your Inner Leader has begun a journey to live and act authentically while delivering value every day.

PERSONAL BRAND EXERCISE 7: COMMUNICATE YOUR PERSONAL BRAND ON SOCIAL MEDIA

Get your brand out there on whatever social media you use. Remember this is your marketing collateral, and every piece of your marketing collateral should sing exactly the same brand. This means that your profile on LinkedIn should sing the same song as your professional bio that you use for speaking engagements or that is on your firm's website. Your presentations and your behaviors should have the same standards as your project reports and your resume. Your tweets, Facebook posts, and blog entries should all sing the same song about you. Awards given and received should demonstrate your unique promise of value. Remember, it is not bragging; it is concisely and precisely communicating the facts about you. Spend 30 minutes a week getting your brand out there on your social media of choice. This can be divided up into two times a week for 15 minutes or three times a week for 10 minutes. Whatever works for you, commit to doing this. The ultimate goal here is for you to have social media on your brain always: when something good happens; when you have a great presentation, meeting, or webinar; when you learn something exciting about your industry, product, or customers; or when you see an article that you must send or you retweet an insightful note. Always think, *How can I reuse this*? For example, if you do a great presentation, write an article on it, and then post it on several blogs and retweet some of the discussion. Become the master of repurposing your success to keep your personal brand fresh.

You will be amazed at how easy it will become to put your mark on everything that you do.

CASE STUDY

I was recently out on the West Coast and was able to catch up with Chin. It has now been four years since he first built his personal brand statement. The first thing that I noticed was that his conversation was peppered with the keywords from his brand. He is comfortable being a citizen of the world and is embracing his courageousness to build an entire international department with a fabulous staff, whom he is mentoring to build and live their personal brands. Chin's Inner Leader has come forth to shine.

PERSONAL BRAND CHAPTER SUMMARY

- Your personal brand is your unique *promise* of value. It is composed of your strengths, values, target audience, results, and benefits.

- Building and using your personal brand is not a check-the-box activity; it is a lifelong commitment to precisely and concisely telling the facts about you, daily. Doing it often will make it a natural part of you, in other words, a habit.

- Perceptions about you are constantly being reinforced by your audience. If they are good, keep them; if they are incorrect, you must work hard to change them. You are 100 percent in control of your personal brand.

- Personal Brand Exercises 1 through 5: Fill in the template: *I use my (strengths) _____1_____ to do (what) _____2_____ to whom (target audience) _____3_____ so that the target audience does (what) _____4_____ and gets (what results) _____5_____.*

- Personal Brand Exercise 6: Say your personal brand statement at least once a day, and it will become a natural part of your personal communication.

- Personal Brand Exercise 7: Spend 30 minutes a week getting your brand out there on your social media of choice. Become the master of repurposing your messages to keep your personal brand fresh.

- Your personal brand allows you to put your mark on everything that you do.

PART
TWO

Evolve Your Inner Leader

Y ou are now armed with an incredible amount of self-knowledge that you have discovered in Part One. How does it feel to be so in tune with *who* you are and *what* you do? In any situation, with any level of person, and without hesitation, you can talk about yourself in a manner that is succinct, understandable, and powerful. Your Inner Leader is smiling.

Now on to Part Two. In this part, we are going to put all those great Inner Leadership aspects to work. Once you read and do the exercises in this part, you will have the knowledge, confidence, and empowerment to:

- Enhance and effectively increase productivity
- Delegate, not drop, your work
- Work less and do more
- Use your personal language to communicate powerfully
- Understand what a mentor can do for you and how to get one

- Become a networking master and actually enjoy it
- Understand what you want to be known for and begin to build your Leadership Legacy

The exercises in Part Two will be different from Part One's; they will be about changing the way that you work with others. Keep in mind the Change Model (see Figure 1.1) as you look to become more aware and more accepting to make the choice to make the change. Just as in Part One, these exercises will be difficult, and they are designed to help you make the changes that you need to profoundly unleash your authentic Inner Leader.

Go ahead; take the plunge into the pool of allowing your Inner Leader to show. For the first time you might surprise yourself by how much you really have to offer to make your impact on your organization. You will be one of the few leaders who will be ready to unleash your leadership to the world!

CHAPTER 6

Productivity: How Do You Get Work Done?

Techniques for maximizing productivity are discipline, delegation, and energy. The discipline of using your secret advantage means taking the first small step, every time, every day, and taking many steps will begin to create positive energy. For appropriate delegation, use the Great DANE model: Delegate, Automate, Negotiate, and Eliminate. To enhance your delegation ability, delegate a job to someone who has the strengths to do the task; empower others to ask for what task they want rather than telling them and overcommunicating. Also, learn to say no, which will change the cycle of the external world's expectation of you. Finally, for successful delegation, break the habit of doing what others deem you should do. Manage your physical energy, not your time, to give you a positive return on your energy expenditure. Learn to exert then recover. In summary, discipline, delegation, and managing your energy are the key to maximizing your Inner Leader's productivity.

Meet Tamika, a professional recruiter in a very specific market of recruiting doctors for hospitals and large medical practices. She moved to the Raleigh area to start an office, and after eight years her office was grossing more than $25 million per year. She had three teams, each relating to a specific therapeutic area. Tamika already had a very full plate at work. In addition to her current responsibilities, for the past month she had traveled around the country, facilitating introductions of her company's new president.

Upon her return to the office, she was looking forward to business as usual. It was then that the director of her largest team, Jim, announced that he was leaving. She came to our meeting one day very upset at the prospect that the team lead of her biggest producing team was leaving. She was beside herself and was in a productivity crisis. Under normal circumstances she ran a very productive office, her teams always exceeded their metrics, and she worked 70 hours a week. Now with the news of Jim leaving, she was assuming that she would now have to take over the leadership and work production of the team herself. She was overwhelmed and her only idea was for everyone, including herself, to work even harder to get over this productivity bump.

As a business coach, emerging organizational business trends become obvious to me as I work with individuals from different organizations to maximize their performance and make their life better. Improving productivity is one of the top questions that clients ask in terms of maximizing performance.

Work productivity is a big subject, and it can mean different things to different people. To clarify exactly what the individual's productivity issue is, I will ask a bunch of coach-type questions to understand exactly what piece of productivity is the cause for concern. When I ask those questions, productivity improvements or enhancements can typically be segmented into these three areas: (1) discipline, (2) delegation, and (3) energy. In this chapter we will examine all three.

HOW DISCIPLINED ARE YOU?

For most successful business professionals when we talk about productivity, the discussion inevitably turns to delegation. Top business leaders regularly request help with delegation. Does this surprise you? When you think about it, it makes sense because high performers are very good at driving results and to get to that next step of leadership, they need to understand how to stop doing all the work themselves and how to help their team members take on more work. When asked how to improve productivity, I share successful delegation tools only after we examine clients' discipline. Why discipline, you ask? Because one cannot be a successful delegator without being disciplined.

Webster's Dictionary defines discipline as "training that corrects, molds, or perfects … moral character; control gained by enforcing obedience or order; orderly or prescribed conduct or pattern of behavior; a rule or system of rules governing conduct or activity." Therefore, the precursor to successful delegation is successful discipline, self-discipline with razor-sharp focus on your goals. I like to call this concept *your secret advantage.*

The idea of your secret advantage is based on the fact that every day we make many choices. Making a decision with your goals in mind, every time, even on the smallest of things, is what will give you your secret advantage. By committing to make a decision, regardless of how small, this act then moves you forward. Making small decisions will enable you to take the first step that will inch you toward your goal that will ultimately catapult you forward.

Think about the decisions that you made in the past week. Hopefully they went something like this:

- I *will* call that customer who had the product problem to see whether he or she is happy with the resolution.
- I *will* take a solid hour first thing this morning to tackle that difficult budget issue.
- I *will* leave a voice mail for the people who coordinated the meeting and thank them for a job well done.
- I *will* work out today, instead of waiting for tomorrow; I *will* have the salad instead of the cheeseburger for lunch.
- I *will* avoid all interruptions for the first two hours of my day and deliver the report early.
- I *will* take 30 minutes tonight to plan my day for tomorrow.

By taking the first small step every day, and many small steps, you will begin to create positive energy. Energy is truly an amazing thing!

The more positive the energy is, the easier it is to build on it, to duplicate the movement, and to get things done. Every time you have a decision to make, take the high road: Take the single step that moves you closer to your ultimate goal. Be relentless, do not stop, and build on your last positive decision. You will be amazed at how quickly your first steps compound into great accomplishments.

In his book *One Small Step Can Change Your Life: The Kaizen Way*, Robert Maurer (Workman, 2014), espouses the same technique. He defines the Kaizen way as the art of making great and lasting change through small, steady steps. This secret advantage is a great model to follow when trying to make big changes that will last and become a part of you and your organization.

In *Outliers: The Story of Success* (Little, Brown, 2008), Malcolm Gladwell talks about needing 10,000 hours of doing a certain activity to be really good at it. He uses the example of Bill Gates, who as a high school student would sneak into the computer lab at the local university and spend many hours per night learning his way around the computer. (His mother was always worried about how tired he was in the mornings.) Another example is how in the early days of The Beatles, when they would play at clubs in Germany, they were required to play for hours on end with only short breaks. These are two examples of discipline. The way that great performers are separated from the masses is directly related to how disciplined they are about taking the next step, no matter how seemingly small it seems at the time. Continuing on their path will keep them steady against all the outside noise when others are long gone. Being disciplined will be an example to others, and your Inner Leader will be smiling.

THE GREAT DANE

I would like to share a story about myself. At the midpoint of my 23-year corporate career, I did not like where my career was going, and I actually hired a business coach. This was in the era when business coaching was still a very new industry. I had the honor of working with Jennifer White as my business coach, who was younger than I, very smart, and a bit irreverent. Her irreverence came in the fact that she did not accept the status quo from me and challenged many of my assumptions. As a coach, she pushed me to understand what my definition of success was, not just to go for the next promotion in the corporate chain. She also taught me to think outside of myself when it came to maximizing my own performance and the productivity of my team. One of her famous concepts of productivity was the Great DANE approach. In her honor I would like to share that with you now because she passed away on June 10, 2001, after making a great impact on the coaching world

---

Is there a clear path to successful delegation?

Most managers find that successful delegation is, at worst, impossible and, at best, frustrating. Successful delegation takes discipline and when facilitated correctly will save you lots of time. Most of us are so used to doing everything ourselves that it seems harder to delegate than just to do it ourselves. *Delegation is a skill; like any other skill, you must practice it to perfect it.* Delegating tasks provides you a perfect opportunity to grow and mentor others in the organization. This is an opportunity for your Inner Leader to really show through. Working with business professionals who are desperate to learn how to delegate effectively, I give them the same simple acronym that my coach gave me—DANE:

Delegate

Automate

Negotiate

Eliminate

We will examine each of these in turn. By following the few simple rules presented below, you will get the results that you want, the first time and every time that you delegate.

What Can You Delegate?

There are two parts to this concept. The first is to delegate to a person's strengths; don't just drop a task to someone else. As discussed in

Chapter 2, if you are working in an area that uses your strengths, you will be happier and more successful. That is also true of delegating; try to delegate a job to someone who has the strength to do the task.

The second part of the concept is communicate, communicate, communicate. Don't drop. Successful delegation requires that you be very clear on exactly what the outcome or deliverable of this activity is. Typically we are very clear about what the result of a delegated task is, and yet we are not very clear about precisely all the tasks, steps, and unexpected actions that will have to be taken to get to this outcome. The point here is to take the time to ask questions and communicate each step. Because this is so important to delegation success, I want to be really clear; if you do not communicate three times more than you think you should, then you are *dropping, not delegating.*

CASE STUDY

Tamika was truly beside herself. After assuring her that there were other options rather than working herself and her staff to death, she calmed down, and I began asking fundamental questions:

- What needed to be done? In other words, prioritize the team's tasks.
- Who could help? Who on her staff were natural or emerging leaders?
- What parts could they help with? Could Tamika divide the leadership among a few people who had specific strengths?

Being a woman of action, she quickly developed a plan, reorganizing her staff and prioritized tasks. She then sat back, looked at me, and happily declared, "That was great." She thought that the delegation plan was done. I smiled and asked her the following questions:

- Do the people that she had assigned to lead certain tasks really want to do those tasks? Do they have the appropriate skills or strengths?
- Does the temporary leader know what is expected of him or her?

- What will he or she do when there is a problem?
- Does he or she know how Tamika wants him or her to communicate with her?
- How should the team communicate a crisis to Tamika?
- What method will the team use to communicate with each other in general?
- What will success look like in two months? What metrics will measure success?

Tamika quickly realized that successful delegation means that you must have frequent and in-depth communication with the person to whom you are delegating and fight the instinct simply to dump the problem on him or her. Although the loss of Jim was hard, that situation propelled her to understand how to begin to delegate to her team effectively.

Wow, did you recognize yourself in Tamika's position? Whenever our world throws us more unexpected work, I suggest that you stop and think about what alternatives you have. Delegation is one of several tools that you have as an alternative.

The reason that I asked Tamika all those questions is because I wanted her to go back to her team and work through the new plan *with them* rather than her deciding the entire plan by herself. Deciding alone is a *fatal mistake* that most leaders make. They believe that they have to make all the decisions and tell their staff the best way forward. Research has proved that if the leader gives the team members a choice of making the plan and then implementing it, each member will take more than what the leader was going to *give* him or her. Wow, this is huge. As you think about it, you will realize that this is true *empowerment*, allowing others to share decision making among themselves. As we all know, when people are empowered, meaning that they made the decisions, or they chose their work, they will be much more motivated to succeed and will be happier!

If this manner of delegation is so powerful, why do only a few leaders do it? The answer is simple and very powerful—and there are three parts. First, most leaders are afraid to give up control. You run a huge risk by asking your staff what they want to do. Suppose you have a team member who has a much bigger opinion of himself or herself, and you are sure that he or she will fail? What will you do then? Or suppose your team members do not understand or know what their strengths are. They will not be able to perform.

Second, the idea of communicate, communicate, communicate is time-consuming and complicated. The leader needs to become very adept at asking open-ended questions so that all involved individuals have a clear understanding of expectations. The hard questions concerning not meeting deadlines and managing unforeseen crises need to be addressed and planned for. Although this might be uncomfortable for both boss and subordinate and team to talk about—imagine the growing experience for all.

The third reason that leaders do not delegate is because they believe that it will take too much time. How many times has something come up, and although you think about delegating the job, 90 percent of the time you simply decide to stay the extra 2 hours that night and do it yourself? This is because until now we have mostly been talking about crisis delegation. Let's change direction. Begin to think about making delegation a priority, not just for getting work done but also as a professional development experience for your staff. Look for tasks that are done repeatedly, for which it makes sense for you to invest time helping a team member learn them so that eventually he or she becomes an expert at them and can take them over.

Delegation is a tool that many more leaders should be using. By understanding and overcoming some of the barriers listed above, you could easily shed much of your work while teaching and empowering your staff at the same time. If you do not have direct reports or staff, delegation still works in a matrix organization and the same rules apply.

What Can You Automate?

Most delegations fail because the delegate will get too far down the road before checking to see whether he or she is even on the right highway. Though you agreed up front on what this should look like, it is better to check in along the way. If you can automate this check-in process, that is even better. Delegating a repetitive task is ideal because it happens at certain intervals and the person to whom you delegated can do it repeatedly until he or she masters it. Even better, automate part or all of a repetitive task, for example, the task of collecting and compiling sales numbers each month. The up front input of data could be automated, and then the compiling and interpretation could be done manually.

Looking at automation as a tool unto itself, take a hard look at everything you and your team does, and see whether you can automate any process.

Many information technology professionals these days are excited about building apps. I recently worked with a man who automated the company's sales force time sheet system for the iPad. The result was that 50,000 globally based salespeople did not have to wait to get to a computer but could complete their time sheets while on the road with their iPads. If you have someone in your group or company who is excited about doing this and excels at automating processes, ask whether he or she could automate a process for you—the person's creativity could be just what your Inner Leader needs to automate a process.

What Can You Negotiate?

Negotiate the task to be completed. Negotiation, if done correctly, should be a win-win for both parties. This normally starts with a request of you or your team. To execute a proper negotiation, you must ask yourself many questions, for example: Is there a shorter way? Can you start with a higher-level view? How important is the task? Can you do it more quickly if you approach it from a different viewpoint? Can you combine it with another process, task, or system? Can you negotiate this task to someone else or completely away from your world? This last question is important. We all know or have heard of the person who keeps a list of his 10 projects on a whiteboard in his or her office. Whenever someone asks for more resources, he or she points to the whiteboard and asks which project should come off to give the requester what he or she wants. This concept is a possibility in an organization that is siloed and where everyone has an equal interest in all the projects. However, most of us work in matrix organizations where there are finite resources competing for multiple stakeholders' work. In this situation, I have had clients develop a detailed list of questions, along with a metric rating scale, to use as the *gate* or first step toward opening up the negotiation for resources. By asking the same questions of every requester, you will be able to build a reusable negotiation strategy for each request.

Remember, just like delegation, negotiation is not used to say no or to dump a project. It is a civilized discussion between two individuals or groups who are trying to find the best way forward, keeping in mind the reality of each other's constraints. Negotiation is a good skill for you as a leader to learn and put on your personal development plan.

CASE STUDY

After our discussion, Tamika had a lot to think about. She devised a plan that included asking her staff for their input. First she gathered the other two team leads in a room and told them of the situation. The three of them immediately began to identify all the work and functions that had to be performed in the next three months. Tamika was comfortable with the fact that she would be able to find a replacement in the next three months. Once they had the factual skeleton laid out, the three leaders called the rest of the team into the room. Tamika explained that Jim had left and that they were all going to have to chip in and do some extra work. Then she announced that the leadership team was going to try something different. They had laid out the general skeleton of work that needed to be done in the next three months, and the leadership team was going to leave the room and let the three teams pick what pieces of work they wanted to take. The room filled with surprise, shock, and a few questions. Tamika calmly answered them all and when everyone was satisfied, she and the team leads left the room.

After 3 hours a spokesperson announced that the teams were ready to share their plan. When Tamika walked in, she almost fell over. The large wall was filled with hundreds of yellow sticky notes. The spokesperson began to walk the leads through what their decisions were and Tamika was truly amazed. Not only had they successfully covered 85 percent of the work to be done, but also the new temporary leader of the team was not a person whom Tamika would have picked.

She congratulated them all, asked many clarifying questions, and made sure that there were hard metrics and good communication channels. She and the new temporary leader, Lorraine, then committed to share responsibility for the remaining 15 percent of the work. Tamika's Inner Leader was *radiant*. A potentially horrible crisis was now being fixed, and more important, her team was happily empowered with a new leader emerging. Life was good.

What Can You Eliminate?

This last step of the Great DANE is potentially the most radical and potentially the most important. Many of my clients come to me in an overwhelmed state and are desperate to get their work life back under control. As I was writing this chapter, I received the following e-mail from a client.

> Vickie, life has become very hectic and crazy since we talked. Two unexpected trips have consumed two weeks. Due to some issues that surfaced last month on one of my products, I've been pulling 12- to 16-hour days trying to keep the project on schedule and recover from a major setback. I was anxious to do the strengths assessment [see Chapter 2] this past weekend but, my mother had to be rushed to the ER [emergency room]. So, needless to say, my weekend plans changed in an instant. I have more travel next week and I'm going to do everything I can to get through the Strengths exercise before then. However, until we get the issues resolved at work, I'm not sure when I will get back to semi-normal work hours. I did receive the highest job rating the company offers and a wonderful bonus for all my hard efforts. But, I gotta say, the money just isn't worth it when it's killing you!

Does this sound familiar? Is your work life like this? Is it always like this? Do you know a colleague whose life is like this? When I have clients in this situation, I suggest that they take a serious look at what is going on here.

Referring to my Change Model in Chapter 1, the first step is to become aware of what you are doing. Is every task of equal importance? Is each task truly making a huge impact on your business? Are there tasks that you can eliminate from your life? Are you saying no to appropriate requests? If not, what is holding you back from saying no? Does the task truly need to be completed? What would be the worst that would happen if it did not get done?

Asking the hard questions of yourself or others is the first step toward becoming more productive. This is where your Inner Leader can really shine. Once you decide what the task is, the next step is to accept the fact that you have the personal power to do the work or to say no to the work. Does this sound astonishing to you? If you truly want to cull your workload, do the following exercises.

PRODUCTIVITY EXERCISE 1: ELIMINATE THE BOTTOM 30 PERCENT OF YOUR WORK

This exercise is very simple yet hard to execute. The exercise is to determine what work tasks you need to stop doing. The above discussion on the Great DANE gave you four alternatives to delegating. This exercise is simply about eliminating or not doing the work. So let's be ruthless. If you are overwhelmed, simply *stop* doing the bottom 30 percent of your work and see whether anyone notices. Radical? Yes! Doable? Yes! Scary? Yes! Think about all the meetings that you attend; is your presence really necessary? Think about when a crisis occurs; is it truly necessary to drop everything to fly somewhere to work the crisis out? Think about all the customer presentations that you are pulled into at the last minute to save the day. If you said no to the bottom 30 percent of what you do, what would happen?

One of the ways to decide what to eliminate is to review your work schedule for the past two weeks. What did you spend your time on? Was what you spent your time on your high-priority items? The key to this exercise is to review your goals and ask yourself whether every task that you did in the past two weeks brought you closer to *your* goals. Once you do this type of review, you will be astonished to find that many of your work tasks are done because another person somehow decided that you were needed. Although this may be flattering at the time, how does it help you keep your workdays from rolling into 18 hours? Now, make your list of the bottom 30 percent of work that you will commit to not doing next week.

PRODUCTIVITY EXERCISE 2: SAY NO TO ONE WORK TASK PER DAY

Another approach to fixing your overwhelmed work life is to make a commitment to yourself to say no to a work task at least once a day. Obviously this is not meant to be indiscriminant or flirtatious. It is meant to ask you to really think about every request that you get during the day and before your natural instinct to accept the work kicks in—to simply think about your answer. By having the goal of saying no at least once a day, you will have it as uppermost in your mind, and it will break your *habit* of simply accepting every task that comes your way.

A story about saying no. Christopher worked in a medium-sized company that was spread across the United States. He was located at the Midwest headquarters and was the most junior person attending the C-level meetings. He had recorded results of the meeting agenda items for a long time, believing that documenting and distributing C-level decisions was important. When he went on a well-deserved extended vacation, he worried about who would take on the responsibility of taking the notes. While he was gone, he missed three meetings. When he returned, he was surprised that no one had taken any notes of the meetings and no one seemed to be concerned. Wow! I asked him how that made him feel. His answer was that he was doing unnecessary work and was slightly angry that no one perceived that work as important enough for him or her to do it. What a revelation! The obvious follow-on question to Christopher was, What else are you doing that is potentially unnecessary? Within two weeks he had eliminated three other tasks that he deemed unnecessary and found time to do the work that really mattered.

Is there anything that you are currently doing that you could stop, and there would be no or little repercussions?

Right about now, maybe you are shaking your head, wondering whether these exercises ever worked with anyone because you doubt whether you could ever really eliminate work. Bravo for you; pushing back with inquisitive feedback is a great thing. Here is where this discussion really gets interesting. Is it really that you cannot find any work you do that is unimportant, or is it more about how you would communicate to the work requester that you decided not to do their work task? This is especially true when the requester is your boss, a major customer, or a stakeholder.

Whenever I talk with people about becoming more productive, one of the first questions that I ask them is to rate themselves on how good they are at saying *no*. I have found that this is a huge problem with many leaders. They are not skilled at saying no. The result is that they have developed the *habit* of simply accepting work and then justifying it by saying that a person required it or that they are the only ones with the knowledge or skill to do the work. Does this resonate with you?

HOW GOOD ARE YOU AT SAYING NO?

What can be done with a person who admits that he or she has a hard time saying no in an appropriate manner? Many times I have spent an entire coaching session brainstorming with a leader how he or she can comfortably and authentically say no. Some examples of these statements are:

- Thank you for the opportunity to [fill in the blank: speak at this conference, present to this customer, do this report, solve a problem like this]. Rather than me doing this let's discuss who else would like this opportunity.

  _____

- I would be delighted to complete this deliverable and I cannot possibly have it to you until [date when you know that will not work]. Who else could get it to you sooner?

  _____

- My travel schedule is full on [date]. Who else would be suitable for this customer visit?

  _____

- I have made it a policy to [fill in the blank: travel only once a month, do only two customer visits per week, give others the opportunity to grow in this area], so let me give you the names of the three people who could help you with your request.

- I am sorry and I simply have to say no to your request. I would be happy to brainstorm with you to discover who else might be able to help you.

- I have made it a policy to volunteer only in areas that are part of my personal brand. Although I could certainly do what you are asking, it is not within my personal brand.

If you choose to eliminate a particular task from your work schedule, it is imperative that you learn how to say no. Even though you have chosen not to do this task, the rest of the world will still be operating the same old way and *expecting* you to take it on. By saying no you are, in truth, changing the cycle or the flow of your external world's expectations of you. Go ahead and try it; although it might feel awkward at first, you will be amazed at how much work you can remove from your plate.

There is a second piece to this idea of saying no. Many of my clients have followed the exercises in this chapter and, like Christopher, were surprised to find that they were able to eliminate more work than they had expected. That left a void. They were used to running at top speed and for large amounts of hours; once they really got clear on what tasks were important and were not important, they began to feel as if they were not working as much as they should. This is a very dangerous place to be because if you do not break the habit of working hard, you may begin to fill up time with nonimpacting tasks. We often choose work that is not the most important because it can fill a need that we have. That need can be to finish something, to please a requester, or to do a task that we consider fun. The point is to be ruthless with yourself in terms of what is truly important work and what is filler work.

Are you laughing at me right now, thinking that you would love to have this so-called problem? I'm warning you that before you begin to eliminate work from your world, you need to have very clear goals of what you want to do to fill up your time. Time is our most precious asset, and when you find some time, let your Inner Leader fill it up with high-impact activities. Be clear on your goals and what you want to do with your freed-up time. Think outside the box, or out of your own silo, group, or division. Is there a special project that will give you a new experience and help you meet your future goals? Go ahead; identify it and go for it. Your Inner Leader will be satisfied that you are finally taking a proactive approach toward working on the tasks that will bring you a *high* return on your energy.

MANAGING YOUR ENERGY FOR SUCCESS

As mentioned in Chapter 2, finding a work environment that matches and uses your strengths gives you a much better return on investment (ROI) on your personal energy expenditure. If you are doing something that you love to do and that you are good at, it hardly seems like work because the ROI on your personal energy is huge. Conversely, if you are doing a task that you hate, you slog through it and you are exhausted at the end. Your personal ROI is in the negative numbers.

The concept for this section is if you become aware of your personal energy and learn how to manage it, you get more of a personal return than if you just try to manage your time. In other words, manage your energy, not your time. This principle will profoundly enable you to unleash your Inner Leader.

Expanding on this concept of managing your energy, not your time, have you ever noticed how your body, your physical energy, has a very definite rhythm? Have you heard people say or said yourself, "I'm a morning person," or "I do my best work in the evening"? That is one way of recognizing your natural energy flows. Have you ever gotten involved with a new client or project team that holds a 4-hour meeting with 20 agenda items? At the end, your mind is mush and your body can hardly move. That is another example of feeling how your natural energy flows.

Meet Sankar, a very successful accountant who was an expert in his field. After 20 years at the same firm, he began to feel truly overwhelmed. Being a very senior partner, he had many people to delegate to and many people who pulled on him for advice and counsel. Sankar made the goal for himself that this year he was going to make a concerted effort to bring in more new clients and get his commissions to the place where he felt that they should be. He gladly went through the exercises presented above, and he appropriately delegated and eliminated much of his nonessential work; yet he was still having some trouble.

He told me that he had read many of the new business performance improvement books and they all said that you needed to do your most important tasks or big rocks in the morning when you are fresh. He had tried that and came to me very frustrated because he was not really moving forward. Then guess what? I asked him a very simple question, which was "When do you have the most physical energy?" With that question the light bulb went off in his mind. He answered, "Vickie, I am really not a morning person," and yet he and I had been meeting at 8 AM for longer than a year! When asked why our meetings were in the morning, he answered it was because he had been trained to do the important meetings in the morning. His *aha* moment was that he was an afternoon person and was at peak physical energy after lunch. Once he rearranged his schedule to do the most important tasks when he had the most physical energy, he began to exceed his client and monetary goals within six months.

This revelation was a huge learning experience for Sankar. Take a moment, examine when it is that you have your most physical energy, and arrange to do your most important tasks then. You will be surprised at the increased impact that you will have.

On a personal note, I am a big morning person, and my energy dwindles during the day. Therefore, you cannot have a meeting too early for me in the morning, and I am diligent about not meeting with clients after 6 PM. Similarly, when I was working in the corporate world, I would volunteer for all the projects in Europe because I could have calls with them starting at 6 AM my time. Conversely, I always delegated projects with people in Asia to others who were night people because those 10 PM calls always drained my energy, and I was not as effective as I wanted to be. When I was writing this book, I arranged my schedule so that I had my mornings free. Most of the time I wrote from 7 to 11 AM, and I found that to be an ideal maximization of my energy and therefore my productivity.

Another concept of physical energy is the concept that likens our body's physical energy to that of a muscle, which needs time to exert and recover. In this case the sports analogy works well; top-performing athletes are very aware of exerting and relaxing. Between shots on the tennis court or on the golf course or plays on the football field, each athlete has developed an exact preshot routine and style of execution and has an equally developed recovery routine.

As the world gets smaller and we become always connected, I would suspect that most business professionals in today's 24/7 business world are masters at executing or *powering through* endless meetings and projects. This is not good for your performance. The question is: When was the last time you consciously *recovered* from a particularly intense business activity? Many high-achieving, responsible, successful business professionals' answers might not be that positive. I highly encourage you to develop your own physical recovery routine, and Exercise 3 below will help you do just that.

PRODUCTIVITY EXERCISE 3: BUILD A RECOVERY ROUTINE TO SUSTAIN RESULTS

To sustain full engagement and maximize our physical energy, take a recovery break every 90 to 120 minutes. As you begin to build the personal rhythm of recovery time into your schedule after each powerful execution, you will be on your way to sustainable top performance. This exercise is for you to think about how you recover from intense work and for you to build your personal physical recovery routine. Your Inner Leader will be an example of sustainable results.

Some examples of building a personal energy recovery plan might be:

- Having a 10-minute conversation with a colleague or friend about something other than work
- Taking a 10-minute walk around the block
- Doing some deep and slow breathing
- Closing your office door and doing a few easy yoga moves
- Reading a quick article
- Returning a fun phone call

Years ago I worked with a highly productive colleague. After every intense meeting I noticed that he would take a 10- to 20-minute walk. Then just recently I worked with a client who, at the end of our meeting, said that he would walk me out of the building. I presumed that he wanted to tell me something very private; to the contrary, he walked me to my car and then continued. He needed to process our meeting and then recover before he went on to his next task. I know that in today's world of open electronic calendars and everyone being able to add to your calendar, this might seem difficult. Yet, however you decide to show it on your calendar, I suggest that you go to your calendar right now and plan some recovery time.

What we just discussed was short-term recovery. Now let's address long-term recovery. Whenever I am interviewing potential new clients, I always ask where they like to go on their vacation or ask about the last vacation that they took. That one open-ended question tells me mountains about the person. Specific to this idea of physical energy, it tells me whether he or she is able to unplug (recover).

PRODUCTIVITY EXERCISE 4: BUILD A LONG-TERM RECOVERY ROUTINE TO SUSTAIN RESULTS

If you have not planned a vacation in the past 6 months, stop reading and do it now. No excuses, including lack of money or time, accepted.

Make it your priority to plan a day, a week, or more off. It does not matter if you go halfway around the world or stay in the comfort of your own home; you need to make plans to disconnect and recover.

In addition, please make a plan for how you will completely disconnect. If you are in the habit of not completely disconnecting during your time off, see the discussion on telling people no earlier in this chapter. The best lesson that any leader can teach his or her employees is to take time to recover your work muscle—and the leader must be an example of this lesson.

Part of maximizing your energy is to examine the level and use of nonphysical energy in our lives. Living a life of purpose fuels our nonphysical energy. That means living your life in concert with your *personal values.* Many of my clients come to me looking for work–life balance. I tell them that we can work on a mountain of techniques for aligning different areas of life, but the key to fulfillment lies in another area.

To achieve balance in your own life, you must first identify your *personal values* and then build an environment in which you can live by those values. See Chapter 3 for more about this topic.

Cindy was the president of a successful coaching firm. She was always running late and keeping everyone (clients, partners, and colleagues) waiting for scheduled appointments. I worked with her on some intense discovery, and she realized that her number one value was respect for others. When asked the obvious question of how her value aligned with her behavior, her mind immediately kicked into rationalization mode. When clients called, she had to talk with them. Also, what was she supposed to do when her partner demanded to see her? I suggested that for one week she agree to stick to her schedule.

The key for Cindy was deciding on a substitute behavior to use. She listened to her gut and decided that she would summon the courage to be honest. She set her phone alarm and 10 minutes before the scheduled end of a meeting, she would suggest that they begin to wrap up because she has made it her personal policy not to keep people waiting.

That was so empowering and successful for her that she was never late again! It is also the exact formula to sustaining top performance.

Although initially Cindy's challenge seemed to be a time management issue, by looking further into her personal values, she was able to overcome her timing issues while being true to herself.

My challenge to you is to discover your values and have the courage to be truthful with yourself and those around you. Commit to living by these values every day to sustain top performance.

In summary, we see that productivity is a big word with big impact and big consequences. This chapter was filled with many techniques and tips to help you improve your productivity and some pitfalls to be wary of when trying to do more with less. We have also seen that managing your energy, not your time, could be your key to becoming more productive.

One last word: Whatever new skill you choose to develop to become more productive, give it time. You will not become a great delegator overnight; you will backslide into wanting to do work yourself. If you choose to automate, the first try might not be perfect, and if you choose to eliminate, you might have some explaining to do. I told the story of redoing our kitchen and moving the trash can in Chapter 1. Something as simple as changing the placement of the trash illustrates the degree of difficulty in making a sustainable change. Try to improve your chances of success with your productivity change by enlisting someone to help you—whether that be a friend, colleague, mentor, or coach—make your change a team effort!

CASE STUDY

It has been five years since Tamika had the crisis of her team director leaving and first learning to delegate successfully. Since then, Tamika has realized that her values did not match the values of the new president that she introduced, and Tamika has left the organization. She found a new position in an organization where her values were embraced. She has a great staff and is the leader of a special project in which she and her team are tasked to eliminate $52 million in outsourcing costs in the next two years. I recently had lunch with her, and she told me that she uses everything that we had worked on during our coaching engagement! Tamika unleashed her Inner Leader and is at a place that she never dreamed of being. She is in an organization that supports her and gives her the recognition that she deserves, while working an average of only 50 hours a week and maximizing her team's impact.

PRODUCTIVITY CHAPTER SUMMARY

- Techniques for maximizing productivity are discipline, delegation, and energy.

- The discipline of using your secret advantage means taking the first small step, every time, every day, and taking many steps will begin to create positive energy.

- Use the Great DANE: Delegate, Automate, Negotiate, and Eliminate.

- Try to delegate a job to someone who has the strengths to do the task; empower others to ask for what task they want rather than telling them and overcommunicating.

- Learn to say no, which will change the cycle or the external world's expectations of you. Break the habit of doing what others deem you should do.

- Manage your physical energy not your time to give you a positive return on your energy expenditure. Learn to exert then recover.

- Productivity Exercise 1: Stop doing the bottom 30 percent of your work, and replace it with high-impact (high ROI) work. Develop and use your method of saying no.

- Productivity Exercise 2: Say no to at least one task per day. This will break your habit of simply accepting every task that comes your way.

- Productivity Exercise 3: Build into your schedule recovery time after each powerful execution; ideally take a break every 90 to 120 minutes.

- Productivity Exercise 4: Plan a vacation within the next 6 months. Plan and execute to be totally unplugged.

- Discipline, delegation, and managing your energy are the key to maximizing your Inner Leader's productivity.

CHAPTER 7

Mentoring: Helping Others and Helping Yourself

M entoring is the relationship between two people in which there is mutual learning and sharing. Successful mentoring means that you need to have a goal and pick a mentor who has experience in that concept and can help you reach your goal. A mentor is usually not your boss or anyone in your direct department. Having a new mentor every 6 months will give you 10 people in 5 years with whom you have a deep business relationship and who will be able to help you evolve your career. This chapter provides six steps to find and work with a mentor.

Melanie was working to improve her networking skills. One day she mentioned meeting Jan, this awesome woman who was in exactly the position that she would like to be in 10 years, although at another company. When I asked Melanie whether she would ask Jan to be her mentor, her response was, "I couldn't possibly do that. Jan is so well known and respected in her field. Why would she want to mentor me?"

This is the shortest chapter in this book and the one that delivers the most return on investment (ROI). Mentoring is the best-kept secret of all successful business professionals. In this chapter you will be introduced to the concept of mentoring and its practical application.

WHAT IS MENTORING?

Mentoring is the relationship between two people in which there is mutual learning and sharing. A mentor can act as a counselor, tutor, supporter, sponsor, and adviser. A mentor is an experienced adviser who can provide you with insight into office protocol and how to handle sensitive situations. These areas are not necessarily taught in school and are essential to career success. Whenever I suggest to clients that they might want to think about working with a mentor, their reactions range from questions, such as "Whom would I ask?" and "What would we work on?" to more of Melanie's reaction, "I couldn't possibly ask her."

A few years ago, I facilitated a workshop for the master of business administration students at North Carolina State University. The graduating students were looking forward to starting their new jobs, and the first-year students were anxious to make the most of their summer internships. I facilitated a workshop titled "How to Maximize Your Performance in the First 100 Days on the Job," which included six robust steps. Of particular note is the concept of creating successful coalitions, both internal and external, in your organization by immediately selecting a mentor and by never being without a mentor throughout your professional life. Even for those of us who are well past our first 100 days on a new job, this concept is still very valid.

STEPS TO WORKING WITH A MENTOR

The first step in working with a mentor is to decide whom you want as your mentor and what you want to work on. Mentors can be internal to your organization if your goals are more internally focused and can be external to your organization if your goals are more externally focused. For this example, let's say that you are looking to understand your organization and to potentially chart your career course for the next step or maybe a few steps from now.

Do *not* ask your boss or anyone in your immediate department. A mentor should be someone outside your immediate world. It could be your boss's peer, someone in a department where you think you might like to work, a person with organizational longevity, or a person whom you seem to click with or who has fabulous business acumen, and you know that you could learn from him or her. Whomever you pick, be very clear on what made you want to ask him or her to be your mentor.

Asking someone to be your mentor can be intimidating. The best way to overcome that intimidation is to have a plan. The plan is simple. Approach the person and explain what has attracted you to him or her (organizational longevity or business acumen, for example). Ask whether he or she would mentor you, and explain that your expectations would be a 1-hour meeting once a month for 6 months. Then explain your goal (for example, to learn more about the person's department or to explore your next career move). The benefit of this approach is that you work with that person for 6 months, and the last meeting should be a discussion about who should be your next mentor. Most people are honored and flattered to be asked to be a mentor.

MENTORING EXERCISE: SIX STEPS TO FIND AND WORK WITH A MENTOR

Everyone who is reading this book should have a mentor, a trusted advisor, or a counselor to guide you as you move forward in your career. Successful mentoring means that you have a goal and you pick a mentor who has experience in that concept and can help you reach your goal. Here are six easy steps to help you find and work with a mentor:

Step 1 *Find* the person in your company or industry that you most respect.

Step 2 *Ask* him or her to be your mentor.

Step 3 *Agree* with this person on the time commitment for mentoring you (e.g., 30- to 60-minute meeting or call every month).

Step 4　*Explain* to this person the goal of the mentoring relationship (e.g., "My strength is _____ and I want to find more opportunities to use it in my daily work").

Step 5　*Describe* the top three reasons why you chose this person.

Step 6　*Explore together* what success would look like and mean to you in the next 6 months.

Imagine that if you follow this plan, in 5 years you will have 10 people who know you and will help support you in your career. This is truly career gold.

No matter where you are in your career, you can have a mentor or you can be a mentor. Mentorship has nothing to do with age, years of experience, position, or level; it has to do with working with someone who can teach you something. The typical thought of mentorship is a more experienced or older person helping a younger person. In today's world that does not always have to be the case. For example, how cool is it when a younger person is asked by a person of more business experience to help mentor him or her in a new technology? If someone is an expert in something that you want to learn, a mentoring relationship should exist.

In the following discussion I have listed some more specifics about a mentoring relationship:

What is the value of having a mentor, or of being a mentor to others? A mentor can help you:

- Understand the informal politics of your organization.
- In the next steps of your career.
- Through challenging projects or relationships.
- Build and implement a personal development plan.
- By introducing you to influential people.
- Live and communicate your personal brand.

What characteristics should I look for in a mentor?

- Someone who has been in your organization for a while and who understands its nuances.

- A thought leader in your discipline, technology, or industry.
- Someone whose career path is one that you would like to emulate.
- Someone whose business acumen you admire.
- Someone not in your direct management line.

WHAT SHOULD I WORK ON WITH MY MENTOR?

Have a specific goal of what you would like to accomplish with this person, and link it to the rationale behind your choice of this individual as your mentor. You could use the list above as a starting point to determine exactly how you would like your mentor to assist you.

Ideally you should explain your goal(s) and clarify your choice as to why you have chosen him or her for this role when you ask him or her to be your mentor. Also, have an agenda or goal for each meeting. At the end of those 6 months, do not forget to thank your mentor in a handwritten note or with a small gesture or gift as a token of your appreciation. Explain precisely how he or she has helped you and what you intend to do with this new inspiration. You should also plan to check in with this person in the future to keep him or her apprised of how your career is progressing. Lastly, find your next mentor.

To reiterate—by following this process, at the end of 5 years, you will have 10 people with whom you have a deep business relationship and who will be able to help you evolve your career!

CASE STUDY

Melanie was still skeptical about asking Jan to be her mentor because she worked at a different company and was so well known. However, after going through the exercises above, Melanie approached Jan with the question. Jan's answer was "I will not only be delighted to be your mentor, but I would like to have you come and work for me in my company." Imagine Melanie's surprise! That was 4 years ago and Melanie has since doubled her compensation, increased her scope of work by 100 percent, and begun working from home 2 days a week.

Now Melanie's case definitely had a surprise ending. We would not normally think asking someone to be a mentor would lead to a new assignment. She did go to work for Jan in her company, and Melanie quickly found a new mentor in the new company because Jan was now her boss. In summary, mentoring is powerful—embrace it and use it to help you evolve your career. Unleashing your Inner Leader is all about doing your due diligence and then having the courage to ask your potential mentor to build a relationship with you. Business and leadership is built on relationships, so review your meaningful contacts and find that next mentor.

MENTORING CHAPTER SUMMARY

- Mentoring is the relationship between two people in which there is mutual learning and sharing.
- Successful mentoring means that you need to have a goal and pick a mentor who has experience in that concept and can help you reach your goal.
- A mentor is usually not your boss or anyone in your direct department.
- The Mentoring Exercise has six steps:
  1. *Find* your mentor,
  2. *Ask* him or her to be your mentor,
  3. *Agree* on the time commitment,
  4. *Explain* your goal,
  5. *Describe* why you picked this person, and
  6. *Explore together* what success will look like.
- By following this process, at the end of 5 years, you will have 10 people with whom you have a deep business relationship and who will be able to help you evolve your career!

CHAPTER 8

Personal Language: What Does Your Language Say about You?

One of the most important tools for a leader is communication. In this chapter we will examine how your personal language can become an extension of you and help you make the impact that you want. The chapter is full of tools and techniques to hone your communication skills and improve your personal language.

For your Inner Leader to shine through, you must master the art of asking open-ended questions and truly listening to the responses. The simple rule for a business professional is to ask open-ended questions that each start with the word *what*. The concept is that *what* is factual; *why* is emotional. Leaders want to ask open-ended questions that begin with the word *what* to get at the facts and avoid taking an emotional position. This chapter will explore several techniques for using *what* questions.

The second concept in this chapter is to stop using certain phrases in your communication. For example, if the word *but* is used, it negates everything that went before it. It is surprising that subtle changes in your personal language can help your Inner Leader emerge as a strong communicator adept at delivering even the most complicated messages.

CASE STUDY

Meet Howard, a senior partner in a prestigious professional services firm in New York City. Howard hails from the South and his buddies actually nicknamed him Rhett for his smooth mannerisms and easy conversation. But make no mistake; Howard is no pushover. In strengths language he is achievement oriented, likes to work on significant projects, and feels most comfortable in a position of command. When Howard first started his coaching engagement with me, he wanted to be a more effective communicator. He said, "We have a lot of smart people in our firm doing a lot of stupid things. I would like to fix that." Although he never shows it, he physically gets an intensity of anger when someone doesn't listen or does exactly the opposite of his request. His self-diagnosis was that he needed to improve his personal communication effectiveness for his true Inner Leader to emerge.

Being more effective at communication begins with that first step in the Change Model—Awareness. Become aware of when you feel that you are communicating well and when you are not communicating optimally. Once you identify an example of when you communicated well or poorly, ask yourself the following questions concerning this conversation:

- Did I listen?
- Did I really hear what the other person was saying?
- Did I truly seek to understand what was being said?
- If I did not understand, did I ask clarifying questions?
- Did I respond to what the other person was saying, or did I push my own agenda?
- If I did not understand what the other person was saying, did I push my own agenda anyway?

- What percentage of the conversation did I talk?
- What percentage of the conversation did I listen?

As an effective leader, there are many ways that you communicate and mountains of material written to help you communicate better. As a coach, I have found that the following tools are universal in that every leader can apply them in almost every situation.

DO YOU TALK TOO MUCH (AND SAY NOTHING)?

To become successful in today's business world, business professionals need to speak up. They typically have become successful by driving results. Driving results means providing direction, giving instructions, and making requests of people. Does this sound familiar to you? How much talking is enough? How much talking is too much? Of course, the answers to these questions depend on many factors: your personality, the situation, your position, your communication style, and the communication style of your organization, boss, or team. Successful leaders got there because they drive results, and in many cases this means that they talk—*a lot.* Many of my clients are *tell* people; they are used to telling others. For their Inner Leader to really shine through, it is important they become more of an *ask* person. For many this change is very difficult.

A way to begin is to assess how much you talk versus how much the rest of the people around you talk. If your Inner Leader is showing itself, you are listening a lot more than you are talking. In many coaching engagements I give the goal of clients listening 80 percent of the time and talking 20 percent of the time. Those numbers certainly give credence to the old saying that no one ever learned anything by talking. How does one accomplish this? The simple answer is by asking questions. Asking questions gives the opportunity to have a conversation. However, the questions have to be formulated in a manner that promotes conversation instead of giving one-word answers. The questions should be open-ended questions. The way to achieve this is developing questions that start with the word *what*.

A word here to the introvert: Although many successful people are those who have no problem speaking up, there are those who would be very happy letting others do the talking. If you want to get better at speaking up, the technique of asking open-ended questions is *huge*. The idea is that you plan a strategic list of *what* questions for any meeting or phone conversation, and at the appropriate times you ask the questions. This enables you to drive the direction of the conversation with you only having to interject the right question at the right time.

DO YOU ASK THE RIGHT QUESTIONS?

When a business professional wants to ask open-ended questions, a simple rule is to make sure that you structure the question beginning with the word *what*. For example:

- What is your going forward plan?
- What is motivating you to call her?
- What decision would you make from a position of strength?
- What about your idea will help us reach our goal?
- What is the first step to move us forward?
- What is your biggest concern about that step?

When you ask the questions above, you open the space up for a dialog. Also when you ask a *what* question, you are requesting that the answer be based in facts. Conversely if you ask a question that begins with the word *why*, you are requesting an answer that could be based more on emotions, thus putting people on the defensive.

Match the questions above with the questions below:

- Why are you going in that direction?
- Why are you calling her?
- Why are you making that decision?
- Why is your idea so important?
- Why are you choosing that as your first step?
- Why are you concerned about that step?

Can you see the difference in the emotion that is felt by the way that the question is structured? Typically salespeople, consultants, and even business coaches are very skilled in asking open-ended *what* questions. What makes it so hard for a leader to ask these types of questions? The answers are almost endless: Leaders have been trained to be more directive, it is a habit to tell people rather than ask, leaders feel like it takes more time to ask than to tell, or if they have the answer, there is no reason to beat around the bush.

Can you see then that what *is about facts and* why *is about emotion?*

From Howard's perspective he felt that whether he asked or told, his message was not getting through. He felt that he seemed to have the same discussions with the same people, about the same things, repeatedly. It was getting old and he was growing more impatient with this type of circular communication. I requested that for any interaction, phone call, or meeting, he prepare by making a list of six to eight *what* questions. The point was to help him structure the conversation by asking open-ended questions that would uncover the important facts that he needed to make a decision. He agreed to try this for a particular problem that he was facing.

The firm had hired a marketing person, Brad, three years ago, and Howard needed to have discussions with all of the eight senior partners to make a decision of whether to terminate this person for lack of performance. We brainstormed the questions that he would ask each of the partners about Brad's performance and they are listed below:

- What are the top three things that Brad has done for you in the past three years?
- What type of revenue or result did these things gain?
- What three challenges have you had with Brad over the past three years?
- What do you consider Brad's barriers to success?
- What three things need to be done for Brad to meet his goals in the next six months?
- If Brad does not meet his goals in the next six months, what do you think we, as a firm, should do?

Howard held the meetings and he felt that they were much more productive than previous meetings. He was able to gather facts about Brad's performance and eventually made the decision to let Brad go.

We see in the case study above that Howard changed his conversation method. His usual style was to come into a meeting and tell everyone his point of view (that Brad needed to go). Then he would beat the point until he won everyone over and the decision was made.

When he changed his style, his Inner Leader *led* each partner to consider the facts and make his or her own decision. This is true *empowerment,* opening up the space so that the facts can be discussed and each person can give his or her opinion. Howard was open-minded in the case that if one of the other partners could give a rationale of why Brad should stay, he would have considered it.

This idea of giving people room to make their own decisions, or opening up the space for discussion, is also the same concept discussed in Chapter 6. As we saw in that chapter, successful delegation is about asking people what pieces of the work they want and then asking a series of questions to set the rules of delegation. This asking rather than telling makes people feel empowered, and your Inner Leader begins to emerge. The same was true in Howard's conversations with the partners about Brad. He was able to gather information and help empower each partner to make the decision in a logical and factual way. Now it is your turn.

PERSONAL LANGUAGE EXERCISE 1: MAKE A LIST OF *WHAT* QUESTIONS

For every conversation, whether it is a phone call, a meeting, or a presentation, prepare for that interaction by making a list of 6 to 10 *what* questions to ask. Then use them!

Over the years I have prepared a list of *what* questions that I have used and shared with my clients. I have reproduced it below:

- What does success look like?
- What is preventing you from _____?
- What are the top three steps to achieve that?
- What is your biggest fear about that?
- What gets in your way in this area?

- What do you want to happen?
- What is the permanent solution?
- What is the truth here?
- What do you need most right now?
- What kind of support do you need right now?
- What do you want the outcome to be?
- What is the ideal outcome?
- What would that look like?
- What is the right action?
- What is working for you?
- What decision would you make from a position of strength?
- What other choices do you have?
- What haven't I asked that I should have?
- What needs to be said that has not been said?
- What do you have invested in continuing to do it this way?
- What is the consequence that you are avoiding?
- What is motivating you?
- What is missing here?
- What does that remind you of?
- What do you suggest?
- What is underneath that?
- What is this person or idea contributing to the quality of this proposal?
- What is the simplest solution here?
- What does your gut tell you to do?
- What would you do differently if you tapped into your own wisdom?
- What are you avoiding?
- What is the worst that could happen?
- What are you committed to?

- What is your vision for yourself and the people around you?
- What are the three most important things you notice about the present situation?
- What do you think you know for sure and what are your questions?
- What are the contradictions that you are encountering?
- What has surprised you in the recent past?
- What are you going to do to make a difference (impact) in the near future?
- What is the inspiration for your solution, concept, or program?
- What is the most innovative way to approach this problem?
- What support do you need to reach your success milestones?

Go ahead; pick some of these to use in your next conversation, and see how much more factual the interaction becomes.

Advanced *What* Question Technique 1: Ask Several *What* Questions Together

After Howard's success with asking the partners *what* questions, he came to our next meeting very excited over the prospects of how this could change his communication from frustrating to successful. He was excited to learn that there is even a more *advanced* concept of *what* questioning.

The first mistake that people make when choosing to communicate using *what* questions is that they ask one *what* question, the person answers, and then they go back to tell mode. No, no, no. To get the benefit from *what* questions, one must stay in *what* question mode. Below is an example of asking only one *what* question.

HOWARD: Evan, what do you think are the top three things that Brad did for us in the past three years?

EVAN: Well, Brad did introduce us to the Silverberg account and that division of IBM, and he got us on the mayor's council for urban development.

HOWARD: Evan, you have got to be kidding. None of those activities brought us any revenue, and they were all just a waste of time.

What Howard should have asked was "Evan, what was the importance to our bottom line for each of these activities?"

What difference do you see?

Advanced *What* Question Technique 2: Waterfalling

All great leaders *listen*. Listening can be difficult for a *tell* person. By asking *what* questions and keeping the 80/20 rule of listening/talking, you will be forced to listen. That is the whole point. As noted above, asking open-ended questions and truly listening to the answers is *a skill that is going to take some time for you to learn*. Although the concept is simple, the change of human behavior is difficult and will take some time. Do not despair; remember the Change Model in Chapter 1: Awareness, Acceptance, Choice, then Change.

Ask at least five *what* questions in a row before offering your opinion or telling the next step. I call this waterfalling. It is basically leading the person with whom you are talking to come to his or her own conclusions through your expert questioning.

Another example of waterfalling is asking the same question repeatedly. This might seem crazy to you at first, as it did to Howard, and changing the wording slightly each time can help you picture this scenario.

CASE STUDY

As a sales manager, Carol is trying to get her salesperson Henry to be more consultative in his approach with customers. After introducing the benefits of the consultative approach, Carol asks Henry the question: Henry, what could you have done differently in the meeting with the customer to get us to understand his goals?

Henry answers, "I don't know."

Now what does Carol do? Suppose she asks the question again.

CAROL: Henry, let's explore this a little further. What skills do you think that you could have deployed to get the customer to open up to us?

HENRY: I don't know.

CAROL: Reflecting back on the meeting, Henry, what do you think that you could have done to find out what the customer's goals were?

HENRY: I guess that I could have asked more questions.

Bingo! There is something about asking people the same question three times that is magic. Go ahead and try it—you will be amazed at what you can unearth with this skill and a little bit of patience.

The skills that we have been talking about also work with children, for example, the concept of asking the child a *what* question versus asking the child a *why* question. See the conversation below:

MOTHER: Emma, why are you crying?

EMMA: (sobbing uncontrollably) I don't know.

Alternate scenario

MOTHER: Emma, what is making you cry?

EMMA: I left my baby doll at the babysitter's.

Also, the concept of asking the same question three times works very well with children. For example:

FATHER: Travis, where is your science book?

TRAVIS: I don't know.

FATHER: Let's think about this for a minute. Where is your science book?

TRAVIS: I don't know.

FATHER: Travis, you are a smart boy. Now think back and let's try to find out where your science book is.

TREVOR: Oh now I remember. I left it at Liam's yesterday when I went there after school.

Advanced *What* Question Technique 3: Expand or Clarify with Numbers

To recap, the first of the two advanced *what* question techniques was asking the *same* question three times in a row, and the second was waterfalling (asking five *what* questions in a row). *The third technique is to insert numbers.* Asking a question with numbers in it gives your listeners a goal and makes them think past the obvious. For example, asking for the three best things that Brad has done in the past three years sets a goal to find the facts.

When I first introduced this concept of asking for numbers to Howard, he thought it was a little harsh. Once we talked about it, he realized that I was not talking about simply barking out a request with numbers in it, such as "Give me four reasons why this will work." It was more about putting some type of parameter on the question to either expand a person's thinking or help the person sift through all the reasons and talk only about the most important ones. For example, if someone is fixated on one solution and has blinders on, try asking, "What other three solutions might we look at to be sure that we have chosen the best one?" This then forces him or her to expand his or her thinking, with a goal of 3, not 10, more solutions. Conversely if someone has a list as long as his or her arm of what solution would be best, asking the question "What are the top three solutions that you would propose?" can help to narrow this person's thinking.

Advanced *What* Question Technique 4: End with a Question

The fourth and final advanced technique for asking *what* questions is to end a conversation with the question. For example, at the end of a conversation, you could ask, "What is the biggest thing that you are taking away from our conversation today?" This is a powerful way to solidify a discussion. If the person took away what you wanted him or her to take away, then answering this question reinforces that take-away. However, there are times when a person will answer something that could be a surprise to you. It might have been a small sidebar or a seemingly insignificant fact that really caught his or her attention. In that case you never would have known this to be important to him or her if you had not asked the question.

At this point you might have some feedback that is similar to Howard's feedback. He was very skeptical and said, "Although I am a skilled accountant and asking questions is part of my toolbox, some of the techniques that you are suggesting seem to me like I might be badgering the person that I am having the conversation with." My answer to that is that taken at face value, like asking the same question three times, this technique will definitely feel like badgering unless there is some finesse involved. Notice some of the examples above. Once softening words surround the questions, the conversation becomes more normal.

In conclusion to this section of four advanced what *questions, asking* what *questions is a leader's gold currency for all aspects of your life. Becoming an expert in asking open-ended questions enables you to get deeper into the facts and provides a venue by which you are forced to listen. When you lose the* tell *and increase the* ask, *your Inner Leader will surface.*

IS YOUR PERSONAL LANGUAGE SABOTAGING YOUR EFFECTIVENESS?

The final part of this chapter on personal language is to take a hard look at exactly what words and phrases you use that might be sabotaging your effectiveness.

No matter who you are, where you come from, how educated you are, or where you work, you have a pet phrase or phrases that are part of your oral and written communication. My question to you is: "What pet phrase are you using in your communication that is sabotaging you and you don't even know it?"

Last week Jon arrived at our coaching session breathless and disgusted about the meeting that he had just left. In the first 4 minutes of our conversation, he used the phrase "I am just so tired of _____" at least 10 times. When I inquired how he thought his listener reacted to that phrase, he looked at me with a horrified expression. He realized that every time he used that phrase, he was sabotaging himself, his effectiveness, his clarity, his values, and even other people's trust in him.

Following is a list of phrases from daily conversation that are very harmful to the most important person in the world—*you* the speaker:

- "You are right but … "
- "I agree with you but … "
- "Yes, but don't you think … "
- "I'm sorry to interrupt but … "
- "You just don't get it"
- "Oh, I was just going to say … "
- "Oh, it was just … "
- "Well in my experience … "
- "I am so tired of … "
- "Well it's about time that … "
- "Well if it were me … "
- "This is ludicrous."

Do any of these sound familiar? What are your listeners' reactions to these phrases? We all fall into patterns of behavior and use catchphrases that become a part of our personal vernacular; the focus here is to pinpoint those phrases that are inevitably sabotaging your communications efforts. When you use a phrase repeatedly, particularly one that has a bit of criticism or edge to it, the result is that you shut down your listener altogether and effectively neutralize your message.

PERSONAL LANGUAGE EXERCISE 2: CHANGE YOUR FAVORITE PHRASES

Now for your exercise: Ask at least 10 people—business colleagues, friends, and yes, even family members—the following five questions:

1. What one phrase do I always use that you would like me to change?
2. When I say that phrase, what reaction do you always have?

3. Can you give me five examples of a different way that I could say this?

4. If I used your suggestion, how would that change your reaction to what I say?

5. What could you do to support me to change this part of my communication?

I have seen worlds turned upside down with the simple change of a phrase. Asking for feedback, especially on your communication style, is not easy. Yet, I encourage you to complete this exercise. Making these small changes will yield huge results.

THREE TIPS TO EFFECTIVE PERSONAL COMMUNICATION

In my years of coaching business professionals to improve their performance, my ears have become very attuned to the way in which they speak and the words that they use. I listen intently to words in a conversation, and I have a radar for keywords that sabotage a person's effectiveness.

Below are three tips for effective personal communication.

Tip 1: Banish the Word *Just* from Your Vocabulary

By using this word as filler, you will immediately subjugate your effort, leaving your listener with the impression that *you* feel what you've done is not enough or significant. See the examples below:

- That is *just* my opinion.
- I *just* wanted to say ...
- Oh, it was *just* a negotiation meeting.
- We were *just* working on the national sales plan.
- My greatest accomplishment was *just* the big sale to IBM.
- I *just* have a master's degree.

My boss and I attended a presentation my peer gave a few years ago. The woman giving the talk seemed competent and imparted some useful information. What I vividly remember is the reaction that my boss had at her closing comments. When she finished what was considered a successful talk, her last sentence was "And this is just my opinion." I remember my boss being extremely upset and explaining to me that with that final phrase she had destroyed all the credibility that she had built up over the past 30 minutes. It had never occurred to me that one small word—*just*—could so negatively affect a listener. We English-speaking people use the word *just* a lot—try going for one week without saying it. This was such a strong lesson that even though it was years ago, I never forgot it; to this day I cringe when I hear a smart person subjugate himself or herself with one simple word.

Since that time I have been acutely aware of how many times the word *just* is used in conversation. It is sad that women tend to use the word *just* much more than men do. The next time that you are at a conference or a meeting, and a woman stands up to ask a question or to make a comment, at least 50 percent of the time, she will start by saying, "I just wanted to say," "I just have a question," or "I just want to ask." What makes us believe that we need to be so demeaning to ourselves? Don't we have a right to be in this place and ask our question? Yet we telegraph though our language and one little word that we do not believe that we have a place at the table. Please become aware of your language and stop using the word *just*.

Tip 2: Never Use *but;* Always Use *and*

The word *but* negates anything before it. When you say, "That is a great idea, but ... " you are really saying that it is not a good idea. When you say, "I agree with you, but ... " you are really saying that you do not agree and will go on to say why. This tip is imperative in negotiations. You would never want to say, "This is a great offer, but ... " The appropriate response is "This is a great offer and there is only one item that we need to close on." Again, this is one of those tremendously subtle word inferenes that once you become aware of them, you will be amazed at how many times even the best communicators will use them. A simple *but* by your boss or stakeholder could tell you volumes about what he or she really thinks of your idea or your work. I find that this tip even works with children. How many times do we tell a child, "This is a great idea, but ... "

Instead let's train ourselves to say, "Maria, that is a great idea, *and* we simply have to ask for Mommy's permission."

Make an effort to notice every time that you use the word *but,* and analyze whether that was the appropriate word for that situation.

Tip 3: Banish the Word *They* from Your Vocabulary

I encounter folks all the time who have simply become lazy and use the word *they* for everyone in every situation. Do you hear yourself saying things such as the following?

- They don't care about employees anymore.
- They said that the plane would be 30 minutes late.
- They refuse to do anything about my problem.
- They had not done their homework and wasted an hour of my time.
- They are always late.

Using *they* makes your communication sound nebulous and imprudent. Contrast that with the use of a proper noun or an actual name, and your communication is more factual and accurate. For example:

- Since Ms. Jones and the new board came to power, it seems as if employee needs are not taken into consideration.
- The senior ticket agent at the gate said that the plane would be 30 minutes late.

- The call center agent named John refused to do anything about my problem.

- David, the sales manager for the Nabisco account, came to the meeting without his team's sales numbers for the month of December. Without this data, the meeting was a waste of time.

- The service team is always late.

By deploying these tips and completing the exercise of asking your friends and colleagues to help you sharpen your personal communication, you will stop sabotaging your effectiveness and will become a more powerful communicator. Communication is one of the most important aspects of unleashing your Inner Leader. Vow to use these tips and exercises presented in this chapter to maximize your communication and let your Inner Leader shine through.

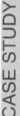

CASE STUDY

Howard diligently followed all the suggestions and exercises in this chapter. In six months his personal frustration and stress level had decreased by 75 percent. His personal language had become precise, and he is uncovering facts that others have responsibility for and having them take ownership of them. He is now able to give leadership guidance by asking factual, open-ended questions and is delighted at the growth of his staff and colleagues. An added benefit for Howard was that he began to use these personal language techniques with clients and prospective clients. Rather than leaving a meeting agenda to chance, he now begins every client meeting by asking, "What would you like to accomplish in this meeting?" Then he asks clarifying follow-up questions so that he is sure to hit the client's goal every time. In the past six months he has singlehandedly brought in 13 percent of the new revenue for the firm. Howard's Inner Leader is smiling.

PERSONAL LANGUAGE CHAPTER SUMMARY

- For your Inner Leader to shine through, you must master the art of asking open-ended questions and truly listening to the responses.

- The simple rule for a business professional is to ask open-ended questions that start with the word *what*.

- What is factual; *why* is emotional. Leaders want to ask open-ended questions that begin with the word *what*.

- Personal Language Exercise 1: Make a list of *what* questions. For every meeting, phone call, and interaction, prepare 6 to 10 *what* questions.

- Advanced *What* Question Technique 1: Ask several *what* questions together. Ask five *what* questions in a row; do not be tempted to revert to a *tell* posture.

- Advanced *What* Question Technique 2: Waterfalling. Ask the same *what* question three times to really drill down and open up the space for an honest answer.

- Advanced *What* Question Technique 3: Expand or clarify with numbers. Ask *what* questions with numbers in them.

- Advanced *What* Question Technique 4: End with a question. End conversations by asking a question, for example, "What was the biggest thing that you took away from our conversation?"

- Understand how your personal language is sabotaging your effectiveness by identifying and not using your favorite phrase as filler.

- Personal Language Exercise 2: Change your phrases. Ask at least 10 people to help you identify the phrases that hurt your communication effectiveness. Stop using them or change them.

- Effective Communication Tip 1: Banish the word *just* from your vocabulary.

- Effective Communication Tip 2: Never use *but;* always use *and*. When the word *but* is used, it negates everything before.

- Effective Communication Tip 3: Banish the word *they* from your vocabulary. Instead of *they* insert a proper noun or name to keep your communication factual and accurate.

- Effective personal communication will reduce personal frustration and increase effectiveness in leading others and achieving your goals.

CHAPTER **9**

Career Evolution: Where Are You Going?

eople need to hone their career evolution skills just like they hone the rest of the skills in their toolbox. The truth is that no one else is as vested in your career as you are and it is your responsibility to evolve your career to let your Inner Leader shine.

The single most important tool for evolving your career is networking. Strategic networking is a powerful career-maximizing tool, especially when done correctly and appropriately. In this chapter we will learn that telling your CAR stories while networking or interviewing is the best way for others to know who you are and what you do. You will learn that there are differentiating factors that will help you stand out and show your Inner Leader to the world.

Meet Rachel, a senior director in a global information technology company. I worked with Rachel years ago when she was in a painful career transition, and when I look at her today, I marvel. Once Rachel's arduous career transition ended on a positive note with her current employer, she decided to give back. Her idea was to network with senior-level executives to get permission to tell her story under the auspices of the company's women's networking group. It took her two years and when she finally found an executive who would sponsor her, she contacted all the experts who helped her through that last big career move and put together a program called The Women's Reinvent Yourself Series. As a project manager by nature, she gathered all her resources, made a timeline for each resource to speak, invited them, and advertised the program internally. I was honored to be one of the 10 outside experts whom she invited to the program. The day that I spoke, more than 90 people were in the room physically or virtually. Rachel produced this series for 2 years, and then the Connected Women of North Carolina asked her to take this series to a larger stage.

The title of this chapter could have been any number of things. If it were named "Career Transition," only folks in career transition would read it. If it were named "Career Development," only human resources types would read it. If it were named "Career Transformation," only people who really wanted to take a risk would read it. If it were named "Career Leadership," then only people who lead teams would read it. So, I settled on "Career Evolution." The point is that *no one* else has the job or responsibility of evolving your career and where it is going. *You* are the only person whose job it is to build your career. If you do not spend the time and effort to build your career, not much will happen with your career. Of course, you can enlist help along the way, but make no mistake; *no one* really cares where your career is going—except you.

It has been my experience that moving a career forward, regardless of where you are in your career timeline, is when your Inner Leader is tested, thwarted, and rewarded. It is also typically a very stressful situation. Why is that? The answer lies in the fact that psychologists have studied the top most stressful situations that humans go through, and making a change in your career is one of the top stressors along with other life changes, such as births, deaths, marriages, and divorces. When you think about it, making a change in your career encompasses each of these traumas: You birth something new, you have a death to your old world, you marry new alliances, and you leave some of the people who are close to you. No wonder it is hard for some people to make a change—even when they are in a bad or impossible situation.

What makes managing, developing, pushing, or evolving our career forward so hard? The answers that I have heard from clients lie in any number of areas, such as, *I don't like where I am, but ...*

- It is safe.
- I do not have the time to make a change.
- I am determined to wait until circumstances will allow me to make a change.
- The industry that I am really passionate about is not hiring and is subject to more layoffs.
- I will never get another job because I do not have the education, experience, or qualifications that they want.
- I am the breadwinner; my family cannot go without benefits.
- The risk of leaving is just too great.

How many people do you know who are truly happy in their jobs? Be honest. My experience is—not many. What makes this number such a huge percentage? This question has haunted me and made me curious for a long time. The answers are varied. People do not leave their jobs because:

- The comfort factor outweighs the discomfort factor.
- When uncomfortable in a job, people tend to dig in and work harder, leaving no time to make a change.
- They rationalize that things are not so bad rather than making an active choice.
- The risk of change is just not worth the reward of the change.
- They are just plain scared of the unknown and change is very difficult.
- They are not prepared and do not have the skills to look for another job.

How sad is that? More often than not, I see fabulous people, with limitless potential and great value, who become stuck in their current situation (job, industry, company, level, or function) because they are just not prepared to take the risk to explore what is out there. The last bullet above is also very true, that people do not hone their career evolution skills like they hone the rest of the skills in their toolbox. This is a shame and I hope that after you read this chapter you will look at your options in a different light.

One other comment: Over the years I have found that company policies have thwarted people from even exploring different possibilities within their career. Have you ever done the following, had your boss find out, and then had an awkward conversation?

- Applied for another job and your boss found out?
- Had a conversation with another person of power and your boss found out?
- Attended an industry conference, had an interesting conversation with a competitor, and your boss found out?
- Volunteered for a special project in another department and your boss found out?

What is wrong with the way that this type of external reach is looked at? What is wrong is that many company processes (either formal or informal) make it mandatory that if you apply for another job internally, your boss will be notified. How does that policy help ensure that people can take control of their careers? It does not! It may also thwart any interest in looking for a job externally because the policy is so tight that one is afraid to be looking externally.

If employees look for another job and find one that they like better, then they should take it because they will be happier. If they look for or apply for another job and do not get it, then they should be happier to stay where they are. Either way it is a win-win situation.

Therefore, your Inner Leader should not punish people who look for another job, nor should your Inner Leader be fearful of looking for another opportunity for yourself.

Many of my clients who are very successful do not have a career evolution plan. They had one at one point, they made it to a certain level, and then they either simply stopped or got complacent. I cannot tell you how many times I have asked a client about their next big move and gotten pushback, such as:

- I would really like to make a change and go to a consumer products company, which is where my passion lies, but when you look into the future, people can do without a new brand of upscale coffee; but they will not be able to do without their medications, so I think that I will stay in the pharmaceutical industry.

- I would really like to make a change to being the executive director of my son's charter school. I have so many ideas of how to make it great, but the salary is about half of what I am making now.

- I am not crazy about working in the financial industry in New York, but the money is so good that I cannot leave.

- If I were to do anything else at all, I would teach at the college level, but if I leave in the next six years, I leave seven figures on the table.

Understand that I am not advocating throwing away a fabulous salary, benefits, and lifestyle for pure passion, *but* I believe that people are not willing to examine the alternatives deeply enough. We are caught up in what we do now for the return on investment (ROI) that it gives us, and we are simply not willing to examine what the change risk really entails. Then what happens? Let's answer that with a story.

I worked at Right Management, one of the top three global outplacement firms, for eight years. During that time the economy went through some drastic corrections, and many of the companies in the Research Triangle Park where I live in North Carolina let lots of people go. I had streams of executives coming through my office weekly who had worked at the same company for 18, 22, or 26 years and did not have the first clue about looking for a job because the only jobs they had ever had to look for were internal, where they were a known quantity.

That is when I really began to study the qualities of an Inner Leader that helped individuals make it through this terrible time. In a situation like this you are stripped of all the trappings of your former life, not only your salary and benefits but also your title, your ability to make an impact, and your self-esteem. I could fill this whole chapter with stories and lessons that I learned from that time, yet I will make only one main point. All the excuses about why you are not looking for your next job now are seemingly valid when you are saying them, but you allow others, the almighty *they*, to make your career decisions for you.

If you really want to unleash your Inner Leader, you must take control of your career today and in the future. After reading Part One of this book, you now know your strengths, values, CAR stories, and personal brand and are more ready than you think to examine your alternatives much more closely.

WHAT IS YOUR NEXT STEP?

Whenever people come to me and say that they are ready to begin to think about the next step, I tell them the three phases of career evolution in the following analogy:

Phase 1   *Discover your story.* Imagine that you are a product. For you to get to the next step, what must we do with this product that we call you? As when introducing any new product into the marketplace, there are three phases. Phase 1 is to discover the story by getting to know the product; what are its features, benefits, target audience, price point, and value to the purchaser?

Phase 2   *Market yourself.* Once we have your story, then phase 2 is to build a marketing plan; for example, who needs this product, who are the end users, who is the purchaser, who is the target market, is there a secondary market, what is the price point, who is the competitor, what is the competitor's price point, what are the product's differentiators, and how do we advertise this product? Once the marketing plan is built, then part of phase 2 is that it must be implemented. Whether you are looking to make a change internally or externally you must market yourself.

Phase 3 *Interview Process*. Finally phase 3 is to be selected through the interviewing process, which in some companies can be very extensive. In this chapter we will examine each of these steps and of course, give you some exercises.

CASE STUDY

I met Rachel while I was working at Right Management. She had been let go from her previous job and was devastated. Although she did not share her personal life immediately, I found out later that she had just gone through a divorce and moved houses and because of those extra expenses did not have much money. In essence she *needed* a job. Being the maximizer that I am, we had discussions early on about simply getting a job or taking the time and looking for the *right* job. Rachel agreed that because she was in such a time of transition in her life, she would take the time and follow my plan. She embraced the plan and even had some self-discoveries along the way.

SUCCESSFUL CAREER EVOLUTION PROCESS PHASE 1: DISCOVER YOUR STORY

This first step is all about getting to know yourself (the product) and then building all your marketing collateral so that everything screams the same message about you. If you did the exercises in Part One of this book, you have already unleashed your Inner Leader, and you are very familiar with yourself. Also, if you did the exercises in Part One with enthusiasm, then you have been telling others about you (your strengths, values, impact, and personal brand), so you are a known entity both internally and externally.

Think about this—when someone is interested in buying you, so to speak, he or she wants to know two things about you: *who* you are and *what* you do. The only way that someone can gauge your future performance with him or her is to ask you to prove your past performance. For some this can be very daunting. For those who have done their CAR stories (see Chapter 4), this is easy. Remember, your CAR stories are your career currency; they are facts of your impact to your organization that never change and that you have forever.

Learning to talk about your impact in the form of CAR stories is vital to your career evolution.

The second thing that people want to know about you is *who* you are. This means what drives and motivates you to make the impact that you do. In essence, what are your strengths, values, and personal brand? For career evolution, I recommend that you determine three key phrases or concepts to describe yourself and use them consistently to complete your presentation of you.

What Is Your Story?

Volumes have been written about career evolution, and in this chapter, it is all about unleashing your Inner Leader to the world. The first phase of career evolution is to have a story.

I enjoy watching spy television shows, and one episode really stuck with me. The story and the outcome were predictable: Three American hostages were taken by foreign pirates who demanded ransom. At the headquarter offices, the two people in charge turned to the rookie for the final decision. Of course she made the correct decision and the hostages were rescued.

The scene that affected me most was the conversation at the end between the bosses and the rookie. As the rookie was gushing her thanks for being allowed to help with the decision, one boss wisely told her, "Today is one of your stories; you already have many stories from your rookie year. And you will have more stories while you are working for me ... someday then, *you* will be the story."

This made me think about the stories of our careers and brought to mind the following questions:

- What is your story?
- How do you tell your story?
- Whom do you tell your story to?
- Who hears your story?

We will answer the first two questions about your story now and save the last two questions for phases 2 and 3.

Career evolution is always based on doing your job well and getting great results. But it does not end there. Being able to step back from your daily activities and get a picture of *who* you are and *what* you do is essential. Then, the real magic happens when you learn how to tell others your story. As discussed in Part One of this book, telling others your story is very hard to do because we are not built to talk positively about ourselves and all the cultural rules say we should not talk positively about ourselves. Once again, you do yourself (and others) a disservice by *not* telling them about you.

When thinking about your story, ask yourself the following questions and write your answers down:

- What is it that sets me apart from my peers?
- What strengths do I use to drive results?
- What are my biggest success stories?

As discussed in Chapter 4, once you wrote your CAR stories, did any patterns emerge? What do you consistently do? What strengths and skills do you consistently deploy? What impact do you consistently have? For example:

- Do you have the skill to see a problem before it really becomes a problem?
- Are your solutions to problems very innovative—no ho-hum for you?
- Are your relationships the primary drivers of your results?
- Can you develop a plan that takes into account all contingencies so that there is little risk?
- Are you the leader who can empower your team to try something new and succeed?

By identifying these patterns, you can get back to your core strengths by realizing what you are good at, and then you can look to do more of that in the future. Your stories will not only become part of the foundation for your personal brand they are also the building blocks for your networking activities. Everyone loves to hear a story, and we sometimes discount our stories as not interesting to others—not true. Practice your stories and enjoy sharing your stories as you connect with others.

Carl is a great example of someone who could not see his patterns after writing his CAR stories. After much discussion, it turns out that he had several CAR stories where he or his team kept running into obstacles, and he was able to turn those obstacles into positive results. It seems that telling Carl's story might be helpful to those who are struggling with discovering their stories.

Carl had developed a process for adding approval of countries that his new software would support. The process called for adding countries once a year, and it had been running smoothly for five years. Enter a new international product manager who wanted to circumvent the process and add two more countries immediately. Rather than fighting him, Carl negotiated with him that the product manager's team could do all the prep work and together they could meet with the inside and outside counsels to get the approval. The result was that the product team got what it wanted and absorbed the work and cost, whereas Carl's process stayed intact. A win-win for both parties.

When I asked Carl to put a name to the skill that he used to alleviate this obstacle, he could not. I suggested to him that the strength that he used was very much that of a strategic activator. As he told me of yet another CAR where he removed an obstacle, this strength came even more into focus.

Carl was part of a large team that was launching a new complex software product. The team had a very specific plan of how the software would be allowed to be loaded on specific hardware platforms. From the back of the room came the suggestion that this software be loaded on the iPad. The entire team knew that this was crazy because the software was so robust that the iPad would use only a fraction of its applications. Carl immediately saw the market for the software on the iPad and told the team that he would take personal responsibility for making this happen. In three months the iPad application was introduced, and sales of the new software doubled their projections. This is yet another example of Carl's innate strategic activation strength.

Carl's nature does not allow him to believe in obstacles; instead he examines obstacles and strategically devises a plan to work with them and find a solution. Carl is a strategic activator and these are his stories that he tells people.

I would now request that you ask yourself the following questions:

- Do you have a Carl in your group?
- Have you worked with a Carl in your past?
- Are you a Carl?
- Do you want a Carl in your group, and if so, how would you find a Carl for your group?

In summary, by taking the time to develop and tell the stories of your success, you can begin to see the patterns of strengths that emerge. By you and your team constantly telling your stories, others can easily identify what the needs of the situation are and who might have the innate strengths to fulfill these business needs.

Are you are beginning to see how personal differentiation can be the tool by which you show yourself and your uniqueness in the stories that you tell? Telling your stories while networking will help others understand *who* you are and *what* you do.

SUCCESSFUL CAREER EVOLUTION PROCESS PHASE 2: NETWORK

In Phase 2 the biggest concept that we need to understand is that there are only three ways to get a job:

- Through networking
- By applying for the job
- By working with a recruiter

Those few people who are really good at evolving their careers are always on the lookout for opportunities to network and opportunities to hear about new jobs.

Networking is a huge component of unleashing your Inner Leader. Business is built on relationships and relationships are built on people engaging in a one-on-one situation. Leaders know people and people know leaders. Relationships are a two-way street and even for the most introverted, relationships are still essential to your career evolution. If you are looking to evolve your career internally, then much of your focus should be on building relationships internal to your organization. Obviously if you are looking externally, then your networking circle expands. If you are looking to make a major move to a different business altogether, you must do a lot of exploration networking.

Do You Network?

Networking is a powerful career-maximizing tool—when done correctly. Most business professionals whom I meet do not know how to network. This should be a mandatory class in any school that is preparing business professionals to work in organizations that provide products, services, or ideas. One of the benefits of networking is that in bad economic times or in career evolution times, it can be a lifesaver. Chances are if you are reading this book, you are savvy enough to know that you have to network—yet are not sure that you are doing it the best way possible. Read on.

In the world of psychology, one of the tools practitioners use is a fast-paced word association exercise. The doctor prompts with a word, and the client responds with his or her gut reaction. The feedback in this exercise is immediate and not a considered response; it typically is parallel to the underlying values of the client. So, let me play armchair psychologist for a moment and ask what word comes to mind in response to the word *networking*?

- Exciting
- Drudgery
- Fun
- Intimidating
- Rewarding
- Not being authentic
- Helping others

- Not sure how to do it
- Helping myself
- Personal development

Wherever you are in the gamut of emotions that the word *networking* conjures up, whether you are comfortable or uncomfortable with the concept, bottom line—networking works!

How to Network

Whenever I broach the subject of networking, if people are honest, they frequently have the same reaction: "I am not sure how to go about networking." My response is always the same: "Just like any other business project that you begin, you need to have a goal and a plan."

Individuals network for all different reasons and for many different goals, which means that there are many ways to network. For this discussion, let's focus on networking where your goal is seeking information or connecting.

Let's suppose that you have been working at the same organization for more than five years. You have had progressive jobs, each with more success. But, you really do not know where your next step should be. Perhaps it could be within your current organization, or in a totally new function, area, or even company.

Chances are that you do not have enough facts even to begin to make a plan (you might have a lot of hearsay or organizational gossip but few facts). In this case you are looking to begin a networking project of researching to get more information and make connections. In this situation I suggest the following as a networking plan.

Make a list of 10 people who you believe have information that could be helpful. Ask each of these individuals for 30 minutes. Create an agenda that looks like this:

- Tell him or her about you (5 minutes). Chances are that the person might know you but might not know of your specific past accomplishments. Tell your story of *who* you are and *what* you do.

- Brainstorm with him or her (10 minutes). Asking the person to brainstorm with you will begin to tap into his or her knowledge. Topics could include questions such as: What companies or industries could use what I have to offer? If you were me, where would you be looking? Where in your company would someone with my background fit? Who do you know that does work similar to what I am looking for? Truly brainstorm—that means that you do not say anything except "That's good" or "What else?" for a full 10 minutes. The reason is if you start talking about point number 4, you will never get to point number 20.

- Discuss the brainstorming (15 minutes). Now that you have a long list on the table, discuss with the person exactly what he or she was thinking when saying certain responses.

Your goal for this meeting should be to come out with two new ideas and two new contacts. Making a plan and a goal for your networking meetings will make you a great networker and connector of people. Remember that networking is a two-way street; always ask the person what you can do for him or her.

CASE STUDY

Back to Rachel. She had happily worked at her new job for the past several years; however, something happened to Rachel along the way. She let the negative reaction of a senior manager beat her down—and she worked even harder to prove this man wrong. She picked up the pieces that her immediate boss dropped, and she made her boss look very good. She steadily grew in her job and began graduate school to add credibility to her skills. Then her boss left, and Rachel was not promoted to the now-vacant position.

"What happened?" she asked herself. "I have been working hard for nearly five years. I have gotten good results—why was I not rewarded for that effort?"

She came to me dejected and disheartened *but* ready to take back control of her life. I had one word for her: *network!* Together we made a list of 10 influential people in her life and

made a goal that she would meet with one a week.
Four months later she enthusiastically contacted me with
exciting news—she just got her dream job and a 12 percent
salary increase, and she attributed that dream come true to
the effort she made with her *networking*.

Whatever your current challenges, ask yourself two critical
questions:

1. *Who* do I know who can help me with this problem?
2. *Who* do I know who might know *somebody else* who could help
   me with this problem?

A very successful businesswoman here in North Carolina has the
following motto: *Always ask* who *can help me; do not ask* what *should I do!*

If you believe in this motto and act accordingly, you will be like
Rachel and be in control of your next success.

Networking Obstacles

Are you rolling your eyes, because you are thinking that you will never
have time to do all this networking, do your job, and have a life? This
is a valid point and there is no easy answer. This is where pulling on
your Inner Leader to believe in the value of networking is the first step.

Discipline yourself (see Chapter 6) and build a *smart* networking
plan. Take some time to figure out what your goal is and who would
be the best person, people, or organization to help you in attaining
that goal. One of my rules is to have a goal for every networking meeting. Your networking efforts will be more productive and effective, the
more that you can narrow your goal to the specifics of your meeting.
Some examples of networking meeting goals are:

● In a large meeting, to meet as many people from three specific
   companies on your target list as possible, with the goal of setting
   up an individual meeting with them later.

- To have a one-on-one brainstorming meeting with someone from an industry that you are interested in, with the goal of getting two new ideas and two new contacts.

- In a large meeting, to meet as many people with a specific title in a specific environment, for example, executive directors of medium-sized nonprofits in the scientific space.

- To have a one-on-one meeting with your boss's peer in another part of the company that you are interested in, with the goal of getting two new ideas and two new contacts.

Sometimes people tell me that they are an introvert and cannot stand talking with people. In this situation, once again, your Inner Leader has to believe in the power of networking, and you have to find a venue that is comfortable for you. The suggestion is to start with one-on-one meetings with people whom you know and ask them for other contacts. This way when you meet the second contact, you will already have something in common with them and the meeting should be easier. The story below might be of some help.

When I was working in the corporate world, my coach and I decided that I needed to network. I had just moved to North Carolina and needed to meet other people from high-impact industries. Even though I am a natural extrovert, the thought of networking terrified me, but I believed that this was what I needed to do. So, I dutifully did the research and found an organization that interested me. I left work and drove to the location; the whole time driving there that inner voice inside my head kept giving me a million reasons why this was a bad idea and saying how I could be so much more productive going home and doing so-called real work. Once I parked, I sat in the car for 10 minutes fighting that inner voice, and finally the only reason that I got out of the car and into the building was because I did not want to tell my coach the next day that I had failed. This was my first step toward becoming a good networker.

In the course of the next several months, I met some great people and was then asked to be on the founding board of the local chapter of Women in Technology International (WITI). To this day if there is one story that I could tell to young people starting out in their careers, it would be to find a network that works for them and become involved.

Networking Appreciation

Whether you are happily employed, you are in career transition, or you are looking for a better working situation, please remember one thing—you are in control. You control your networking activities. You control how you show up. You control the perceptions that others have of you.

Why then is it that so many people have lost the art of appreciation? By this I mean, Why is it that people do not display some act of appreciation? Why do people not send thank you notes, either handwritten or e-mailed? What does that say about you to the people whom you have networked with?

When I was an executive coach with Right Management, I worked with very successful executives who had left their organizations, and I helped them through the career evolution process. As we have already discussed, networking is vital in career evolution. These executives did well and all got new jobs.

There was one part of the networking process that these executives seemed to forget—to be grateful for others' help and show your gratefulness in the form of a thank you note. My standard rule is a thank you e-mail within 24 hours and then a handwritten note to arrive within a week or at a strategically timed arrival. One of my most shocking moments was when an executive was telling me that he had an interview; I interrupted him to ask whether he had written thank you notes. He looked at me in total wonderment and answered no. When I asked him what his reason was for not writing a note, his answer was "Because the next action is for the interviewer to take." *Wow,* now it was my turn to be shocked. I suggested that he thank these folks for their time, their interesting discussion on _____, or the fact that they shared interesting information.

Please, when you network, send thank you notes, in whatever format works for you. I have personally tracked the number of people who send thank you notes for interviews for more than a decade, and it never ceases to amaze me that the statistics do not change year over year; only 25 percent of interviewees send thank you notes. Because interviewing is a formal process, the percentage is even lower when tracking thank you notes for a networking meeting.

A note to those people who lead teams, large or small, matrixed or formal—a thank you note can set you apart from all the other leaders in your organization and will make a huge impact on your team. I suggest that you embrace the exercise in this chapter and develop a personal process by which you remind yourself to let your appreciative Inner Leader come out in the form of a thank you note.

CAREER EVOLUTION EXERCISE 1: APPRECIATE THOSE WHO'VE HELPED YOU

Figure out the best way for you personally to remember to write thank you notes. A few suggestions are:

- At the end of each milestone, deliverable, or project, make it part of your process to write notes of gratitude to key participants.

- Pick a date each month and put a reminder on your calendar to write one or more notes to people who have helped you during the month.

- Make it a practice to send a quick two-sentence e-mail after every networking meeting.

- Send a note to internal or external customers thanking them for their business.

- Make it a practice to add a note of gratitude at the end of 50 percent of the e-mails that you send.

Many times I get e-mails back from clients and former clients telling me how they put the advice into practice and what results they achieved. With their permission, I would like to share with you some of these success stories:

- "Vickie, these are great words of wisdom. I have only written a few notes in my professional career and they have always made a big impact on those people. One person told me that in all of his 25+ years of business that was the first handwritten note of thanks that he had ever received. After that he became my best customer. Thanks for the reminder!"

- "Vickie, I just wanted to tell you that about a month ago you suggested that I send one last follow up letter to the district manager at the pharmaceutical company that I was so interested in, thanking her for the interesting discussion that we had the three times that we met. So I did, despite the reject e-mail that I had just received directly from the company. Well, she just sent me an e-mail requesting my resume for a GI [gastrointestinal] specialty position in Raleigh ... yeah. I was amazed that she remembered me and learned the power of a thank you note."

- "I have an update for you. I sent a draft of your newsletter article to the person who, at the time, had been my boss for seven months. He had just accepted another position (our team is going through a lot of downsizing right now). He forwarded it to his boss, who is actually the manager who hired me last summer. She was preparing to change jobs herself and was approached by a business unit manager who was looking for someone who could lead his training and quality effort. Having just received the article, she took my resume and passed it along. Last week I was offered that position and will start next week. I learned a huge lesson ... that is ... we must promote ourselves while networking, because it is the only way to get noticed."

For more than two years I have been working with a contractor to a federal agency. We started with him building concise strengths statements and using them at least once a day. After six months we started adding his successful results statements, and he began to tell people these specific statements as often as possible. In nine months he was given a permanent position. The e-mail announcement came out and others began replying with the appropriate congratulations. Even then, he continued to communicate precisely with others (including me, as shown below) what his strengths are and what his results have been.

"Hey Vickie—Thought you might be interested in my response to a message from our director. I start my new role next Monday and I believe this to be one of the best career moves I have ever made. Many thanks to you and your insightful help in graciously promoting myself in each step in the process. Couldn't have done it without you!"

Following is his response to the congratulatory note from the director:

> Thank you for your kind words. Taking on tough projects is a strength of mine and it was truly a pleasure to deliver positive results in the _____ Program that reflect favorably on the Agency. From Red to Green on the Scorecard in one year! As a Federal Employee I intend to expand on this performance with the _____ Team and other challenging projects central to our future success. I look forward to working with _____ to make sure we knock every project "Out of the Park."

Although each of these situations was significant for the person reporting back to me, there are two underlying concepts here. Any self promotion that you can do, no matter how small, no matter how subtle, no matter how creative, no matter how factual, is critical.

The second concept to keep in mind is that you need to do this more than once and more than twice; I suggest that you target once a day. For we mere humans this is hard. When I received the comments referenced above, even I hesitated and asked three of my trusted colleagues whether I really should share these successes or whether it was too much. Of course, they answered with a resounding yes.

The bottom line is this: You are in control of what people think about you. You are in control of what happens to you in your career. Step up and begin to communicate precisely to your world what you are good at and how you can benefit them and their organizations.

SUCCESSFUL CAREER EVOLUTION PROCESS PHASE 3: INTERVIEWING

At some point in your career evolution, you will have to interview for a job. This activity to most people feels like lining up in front of a firing squad of one or many and having them shoot questions at you. I would like to give you a different perspective. I have a colleague who says that there are no interviews—there are only business evaluation meetings. After all, how many business evaluation meetings have you been in? Probably lots! We do our due diligence in just about every project, job, program, or product that businesses create. So, looking at an interview as an opportunity to evaluate the specifics of this business venture between you and the other person, firm, or organization turns this meeting from personal to factual, a more comfortable view than the firing squad.

Very few people are good at interviewing because it is not a skill that we practice often. This is true of both interviewers and interviewees. One of the most worthwhile classes that a company can offer is a class on how to interview from both sides of the table, including what the interviewer should ask and expect and therefore what the interviewee should be prepared to provide. In keeping with this theme, if you have developed and practiced your stories and have told them many times in a networking situation, you will be a fabulous interviewee.

When you are trying to promote yourself—whether in a subtle situation of networking or in the more formal environment of interviewing—your listener wants to know only one thing: *how exactly you can help him or her.* That is, the only indication of your future performance is your past performance. Fortunately, you can easily convey your past performance in your CAR stories. Below are three steps that you should master to *wow* anyone. By using these guidelines, you will be prepared, anytime, anywhere, to talk about yourself and sound professional and in control. Please remember that your CAR stories are simply presenting the facts of your past accomplishments in a precise and concise manner.

CAREER EVOLUTION EXERCISE 2: TELL YOUR CAR STORIES

Step 1: When using your CAR stories in an interview situation for a formalized job with a specific job ad, pick the top five requirements that the job requires, and match your CAR stories to these top five requirements. Prepare two or three stories for each requirement. You could formulate your interview answers in the following manner:

State job requirement + tell a CAR story

+ ask a question relating to the job requirement

If you follow this simple pattern, you will remind your listener of the job requirement, relate the requirement to your experience, and then by asking a question related to the requirement, ask your listener to make the match again in his or her mind by providing you an answer. This formula will maximize your interview experience.

Please note, if you want to get creative, you can change the order of your CAR stories. Putting the result at the beginning sometimes has a powerful effect. For example, the result first format would look like this:

"I had _____ result to this

_____ challenge by taking

_____ action."

Step 2: Now let's look at using your CAR stories in a networking situation. Imagine you have been trying to schedule a meeting with that important person on your networking list. When your persistence finally pays off, how do you prepare for the critical meeting? The answer is to research the top five needs that this person has and match your CAR stories to the person's major concerns. Speak his or her language by matching your past results with this person's current issues. You immediately help your listener make the connections between what he or she needs and the value you will provide. This method will help you maximize your networking meeting.

Meet Mallory. She had just been laid off from her marketing position at a global biotherapeutic firm. The day that she was let go, she went online and was simply surfing job ads. A competitor had posted one that had her name written all over it. She came to our coaching meeting excited and ready to do anything necessary to get this job. Mallory was anxious to discover her *who* and her *what,* to develop her CAR stories, to get out and network, and eventually to use her CAR stories to interview.

That is exactly what she did; she followed everything that has been laid out in these pages to the letter. Then twelve weeks from her last day at work, she was offered that job at the competitor's organization. Her severance from her previous company had not finished yet! Although these results are not typical, Mallory has become a networking convert. She mentors people in her organization to write two CAR stories diligently every month and to build strength statements to use every day. Then she encourages them to network both internal and external to their organization. Mallory's Inner Leader was unleashed the day that she decided to take control of her career, and she has been wildly successful ever since.

Step 3: Last, for a general type of networking meeting, many people ask me how to prepare an appropriate agenda and discussion. If your goal is to give the other person information about you, then use the following format. Match your top three natural strengths to your top three CAR stories. This is your *who* and your *what*. Being able to tell a business colleague confidently and effortlessly who you are and what you do well by giving him or her a real-life example is the best way to maximize both your time and his or her time in this networking meeting.

One of my favorite organizations in which to network is Healthcare Businesswomen's Association (HBA). Every meeting of the local chapter is filled with smart women (with master's and doctorate degrees) who get it. The energy and the brainpower in the meeting room are energizing. I have been involved in HBA's mentoring program since its inception eight years ago.

Meet Catlin, one of my HBA co-mentors. She worked for an advertising agency that had many local pharmaceutical firms as clients. She had recently gotten divorced and wanted to move back north to be closer to family. She used all the techniques mentioned in this book and this chapter to build her self-marketing plan and then took it a step further. Catlin built a *brag book* that contained examples of the actions that she had taken to get her impactful results. This included sanitized project plans, examples of advertising campaigns, client strategic plans, and screenshots of social media campaigns that she had run. She also created a few PowerPoint slides that represented her unique promise of value that she had delivered in the past. Catlin was so well prepared to sell herself that it took her only four months to get a position in another geographic area that exceeded the one that she left, in terms of more responsibility, a promotion to vice president and increased salary.

In summary, successful career evolution consists of you capturing and telling your stories. By mastering these steps and matching your strengths and CAR stories with the major needs of those with whom you would like to professionally partner, you are concisely and precisely communicating your value in any situation. This is the best way to unleash your Inner Leader and let it soar.

CASE STUDY

Rachel is now the poster child for appreciative networking and interviewing success. Although she has been in her new job for a year, she is not slowing down her reaching out efforts. She has developed a social circle program for women in her company. In this program they meet once a month to mentor each other and accomplish their career evolution goals through networking. In her first pilot group of three women, after four months one got offered a new job, and the other finally got the promotion and salary that she had been promised for more than 10 months. These colleagues helped each other find their own voice and ask for what they wanted in their next step of career evolution. Rachel is ecstatic to be sharing these lessons, empowering her colleagues, and giving back to her community.

SUCCESSFUL CAREER EVOLUTION CHAPTER SUMMARY

- The only person whose job it is to build your career is *you*.
- People need to hone their career evolution skills just like they hone the rest of their skills in their toolbox.
- Getting to the next place in your career evolution is a three-step process:
  1. Discover and tell your story.
  2. Use networking to build and implement your marketing plan.
  3. Interview by matching your past results with the organization's current needs.
- Telling your stories while networking will help people understand *who* you are and *what* you do.
- Have a goal for every networking meeting.
- Strategic networking is a powerful career-maximizing tool, especially when you have a goal for every networking meeting.
- Showing appreciation is a secret weapon that will unleash your Inner Leader.

- Career Evolution Exercise 1: Appreciate those who've helped you. Learn the best way for you to remember to write thank you notes in whatever form you choose. Make this task part of your monthly process.

- Interviews are evaluation meetings and you can answer interview questions best by this formula: job requirement + CAR + a question relating to the job requirement.

- Career Evolution Exercise 2: Tell your CAR stories. When in a formal interview, match the top job requirements with your CAR stories. When in a specific networking meeting, match the person's top needs to your CAR stories. When in a general networking meeting, match your top three strengths to your CAR stories to be able to explain *who* you are and *what* you do.

- Your Inner Leader will shine through when you master the art of matching your CAR stories with the needs of others.

CHAPTER 10

Career Evolution: Building Your Leadership Legacy

Your Leadership Legacy is not in the past; rather the idea is to live it now and in the future. Understanding what makes you happy and fulfilled is the first step to building your Leadership Legacy. Building the habit of asking the question "What does success look like for me?" is a way to ensure that all you do is taking you in the direction of living your Leadership Legacy. If one is struggling with a feeling of uneasiness, the process of journaling could help uncover the root cause of the tension. This chapter closes with examples of the Leadership Legacy associated with each of the case studies we have reviewed in the previous chapters. The goal for this chapter will be to review real-world examples of how those we met earlier have continued to grow into living their Leadership Legacy.

CASE STUDY

Meet Jeff, a successful executive in the publishing industry. He came to me after having a successful year but feeling very uneasy and unhappy. He talked about all the normal bothers in his life; he reported to the chief executive officer (CEO) of the Americas and could never have a meeting without the chief financial officer shouting about something. These executives in turn reported to the global C-level suite located in Switzerland, whose goals were very different. Jeff's team of 200 people had worked very hard this year, and no thanks or recognition was given to him much less his team. He attributed some of his problems to the fact that he was in a dying industry (the print business) and therefore had to endure attaining success with even fewer resources than ever.

What I wanted for Jeff was for him to understand what he needed. We started our coaching engagement talking about what success meant for him, and I asked questions, such as:

- What was his idea of success?
- What would make him happy?
- What did he want to spend the next 20 years of his career doing?
- What was his brand?
- What was he known for?
- What did he want to be known for?

There was no doubt that Jeff was already extremely accomplished and he was unsuccessfully trying to figure out what his next step would be. Without knowing it quite yet, he was looking for his road map to his Leadership Legacy.

I drew an illustration on a piece of paper (Figure 10.1).

Most successful performers were on the bottom line, with good, solid, successful performance. Jeff's performance was on the top line. He had started at a young age to be very successful, and by his mid-forties he had found a position of prominence in his industry. When I drew this diagram, I suggested to Jeff that he was looking for his Leadership Legacy. His big smile told me that I had unleashed his Inner

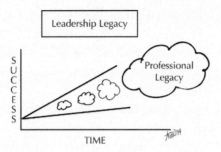

Figure 10.1 Professional Legacy

Leader just with this suggestion. The next question, of course, was how to go about discovering Jeff's Leadership Legacy.

BUILDING YOUR LEADERSHIP LEGACY

After reading the previous chapters and doing the exercises, you are now ready to take your Inner Leader to the next level; that is, you are now ready to build your Leadership Legacy. Most times when people think about the word *legacy*, it is about leaving something at the end. Synonyms are bequest, inheritance, heirloom, heritage, and relic. The question here is:

What do you want your Inner Leader to be known for?

Your Leadership Legacy will not be in the past; rather the idea is to live it now and in the future. It is what you want to build. It is not reactive; it is future oriented. It is about using your current tools to leverage future opportunities. Your Leadership Legacy is about living your brand of leadership with purpose and intent.

WHAT IS YOUR DEFINITION OF SUCCESS?

Let's start this discussion of living your Leadership Legacy with a discussion of success. What is your definition of success?

With the exercises in Part One, you have discovered your strengths, your values, your impact, and your personal brand. Hopefully along the way you have gotten some insights into what makes you happy, what makes you fulfilled, what makes you feel as if you are making an impact, and what your vision for the world is. The next step of this journey is to examine what your definition of success is for *you*. Understanding what makes *you* happy and successful is the first step to building your Leadership Legacy.

"What is success?" is such a simple question, almost rhetorical. Most people include one or all of the following in their definition of the word: to have money, fame, or power; to do the things that you love to do; to be surrounded by the people you like; to be well known, to succeed, and to help others to do the same; to be respected; or to be a hero. Easy. So, if everyone knows what success is, why does this question stop people cold?

Success is different for each of us, and it is different for us at different stages or periods of our lives. Yet there is a thread that weaves through all successful lives, and the word to describe that thread is *fulfillment*. *Webster's Dictionary* defines the word *fulfill* as "to make full … to bring to an end; to measure up to; to convert into reality; to develop the full potentialities of, to make happy, to gratify to the full."

SUCCESS EXERCISE 1: WHAT WILL SUCCESS LOOK LIKE?

When someone is still struggling with his or her definition of success, I typically suggest a few exercises and here is the first. For the next two weeks, every time someone makes a request of you, ask him or her this simple question, "What will success look like when this is completed?"

Many of you may already deploy this technique, and I would request that you now take it to the next level. For example, ask your manager *what* questions (see Chapter 8) until he or she finally indicates exactly what he or she expects during and at the end of this project. Ask several *what* questions in the form of a waterfall until you will have a specific idea of what your team believes will be extraordinary performance on your big project. Document the specifics and continue to refer to this list of excellence throughout the life cycle of the project.

You can also use this technique in a negotiation situation. Before you begin a negotiation, determine what success will look like, and you will have a specific target for your negotiation. Push the person whom you are negotiating with to tell you exactly what he or she wants and what first-rate performance would mean to him or her. This paints a picture of success for both parties.

As another example, when your 10-year-old agrees to clean up his or her room, request that the child explain exactly what he or she will do to make the room spotless. Can you imagine the effect that this will have?

Here is the reason that you want to do this exercise. Once the other party responds to the question, then ask yourself the same question: In this situation, what does success look like for me? What about this situation will fulfill me?

Your answer will be the secret to real success. It will help you define your own intention and enable you to reach beyond your normal limits. Push yourself to look beyond the normal results, and discover the benefits of great performance for you.

To clarify, below are some examples. In each there are two very different successes; ask yourself which one would appeal to you more and what this success would look like if you could do it or live it repeatedly. In other words, what would your Leadership Legacy look like?

- In an oncology clinic
  1. For the chief operations officer, implementing prudent financial strategies, which results in meeting financial goals without affecting employees negatively, over time could be a rewarding Leadership Legacy.
  2. For the medical director, providing successful medical treatments in an environment that gives patients personal dignity, over time, could be a rewarding Leadership Legacy.
- In a 1,000-person call center
  1. Driving results to meet all dashboard green levels, over time, in different companies or industries, could be a rewarding Leadership Legacy.

2. Holding employee satisfaction meetings to understand employees' top three desires, resulting in providing free Starbucks coffee, two nap rooms, and Friday ice cream socials, over time, in different companies or industries, could be a rewarding Leadership Legacy.

- On the board of the local Montessori school

   1. Running the board so that budgets are maximized, ensuring the future financial stability of the institution, over time, in different institutions, could be a rewarding Leadership Legacy.

   2. Holding strategy sessions with both the faculty and the board to develop a five-year strategic plan that focuses on meeting the changing needs of the student community, over time, in different educational venues, could be a rewarding Leadership Legacy.

- In a corporation

   1. Successfully leading the complicated integration of five databases after a corporate merger, over time, in different companies or industries, could be a rewarding Leadership Legacy.

   2. Developing a communication plan where all 10,000 stakeholders and employees are communicated with weekly and are invited to ask questions in real time, over time, in different companies or industries, could be a rewarding Leadership Legacy.

Although the examples above might seem like job accomplishments, if this is done repeatedly, in different organizations and companies, this then becomes a Leadership Legacy. More important, you can begin to discover what your own personal Leadership Legacy might be. If you review your Challenge, Action, Result (CAR) stories that you built in Chapter 4 and look for the impact of what you do consistently over time, you can discover your Leadership Legacy.

This exercise will help you appreciate the gains you make for yourself and help you begin to build a picture of what you want your personal success to look like. Combining some of the previous exercises with this exercise of asking everyone whom you interact with for the next two weeks what success will look like could help you paint a very realistic view of the life that you really want.

Jeff did these exercises and some mentioned in previous chapters. He learned that his personal brand was driving results through compassionate leadership. What this meant to Jeff was that he really wanted to be a mentor leader. He got joy out of helping the people on his team evolve their career and be the best that they could be. To help him live his Leadership Legacy, I gave Jeff a very simple exercise. It was, for the next two weeks, track where he spent every minute of his waking time. This proved to be a total eye opener for Jeff because he spent only 4 percent of his time mentoring others and 96 percent of his time driving results. I then suggested that Jeff stop doing 30 percent of his work. He looked at the bottom 30 percent of what he was doing, and using many of the techniques in Chapter 6, he delegated to his team and empowered them to take on more. Jeff was beginning to build his Leadership Legacy.

SUCCESS EXERCISE 2: UNCOVER YOUR SUBCONSCIOUS

When I introduce this next exercise, no matter what level or function the person has, I always get some quizzical looks. Sometimes when you are struggling with a problem, whether it be determining what success looks like for you or what is making you feel off, I suggest doing some journaling.

Buy a bound book (even a black-and-white, old-fashioned school notebook will do). Commit to write three pages in your journal *every day* for three weeks. Do not do this electronically; something about putting the pen to paper, day after day, unlocks your subconscious. Do not worry about spelling or grammar; you will be the only one who sees this. Force yourself to write three full pages. I sometimes suggest that you might have to start by writing, "This is so stupid but Vickie is making me do it" to fill up the three pages. Trust me, eventually something else will come out.

The purpose of this exercise is to tap into your subconscious, to grab those straying thoughts that keep your mind occupied without your realizing that they are there. Committing to write for three weeks and then reviewing it does not take that much time, and you will discover that the payoff is well worth getting over your self-consciousness about the task.

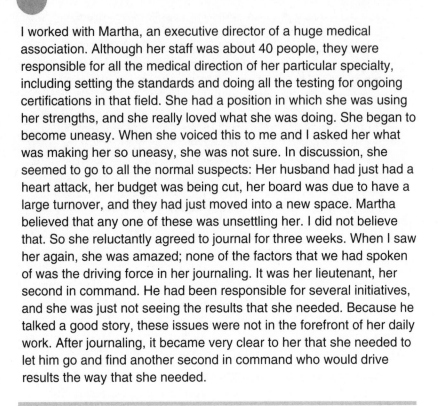

I worked with Martha, an executive director of a huge medical association. Although her staff was about 40 people, they were responsible for all the medical direction of her particular specialty, including setting the standards and doing all the testing for ongoing certifications in that field. She had a position in which she was using her strengths, and she really loved what she was doing. She began to become uneasy. When she voiced this to me and I asked her what was making her so uneasy, she was not sure. In discussion, she seemed to go to all the normal suspects: Her husband had just had a heart attack, her budget was being cut, her board was due to have a large turnover, and they had just moved into a new space. Martha believed that any one of these was unsettling her. I did not believe that. So she reluctantly agreed to journal for three weeks. When I saw her again, she was amazed; none of the factors that we had spoken of was the driving force in her journaling. It was her lieutenant, her second in command. He had been responsible for several initiatives, and she was just not seeing the results that she needed. Because he talked a good story, these issues were not in the forefront of her daily work. After journaling, it became very clear to her that she needed to let him go and find another second in command who would drive results the way that she needed.

What a fabulous way for Martha, and you, to find something hidden that is holding you back from being all that you can be. Asking yourself what success looks like to you, finding a mentor to talk things through with (see Chapter 7), or journaling; are exercises that you can use to discover what in your life is holding you back from living exactly the life that you want and from unleashing your Inner Leader to build your Leadership Legacy.

FIND FUTURE SUCCESS IN YOUR PAST

I was introduced to the book *What I Know Now: Letters to My Younger Self* (Broadway Books, 2008). The editor, Ellyn Spragins, is most recently an editor-at-large for *Fortune Small Business,* and she wrote a column in the *New York Times* for three years. Her book started as an article in *O, the Oprah Magazine* that she later expanded.

Many touching stories from some famous women were sprinkled throughout the book. For this chapter, I chose to summarize two. This selection represents an inspirational message that reminded me of some of the situations that my current clients are facing. Although the exact circumstances may not be a match, the struggle and solution that the pieces exhibit hit the mark.

Joyce Roche, after some time at Revlon, was lured back to Avon to be the first African American woman to be an officer at the company. She was then invited to be the CEO of Girls Inc., inspiring more than 500,000 girls to be strong, smart, and bold. She begins her letter to her younger self by stating that she never set out to be a pioneer, yet here she is breaking all kinds of barriers and being successful. Yet no matter how successful she becomes, the fear of being discovered as an imposter always hangs over her. It is that deep-seated fear that she was never supposed to be there. The threat of failure scared her into working long hours. Yet success only intensifies her fear of discovery. She writes, "Stop. It. Now. You're not an imposter." She assures herself that she deserves a place at the table, so she should relax and enjoy her success.

This story is from Gerry Laybourne, CEO of Oxygen Media. She started as a schoolteacher and in 1980, at age 33, joined the Nickelodeon team and built an award-winning network within 16 years. She left Nickelodeon to spend two years at Disney/ABC Cable Network, and she later made the leap to start Oxygen in 1998. In this role, she persuaded investors to pony up more than $600 million to launch the new channel. In her interviews, she confessed, "I lived a safe corporate existence at Nickelodeon and raising money terrifies me." Gerry wrote a letter to her younger self at the time that she was jumping ship from her seemingly corporate safety to "a Wall Street driven, quarterly measured, corporate culture that hasn't yet bought into your ideas." In the end, her advice to her younger self was:

> "Above all, remember to be your own best friend. Turn off the radio station in your head that points out your failures."

This idea has made me ask the following questions:

- How many of us do not take the risk because of the tune of doubt that keeps playing in our heads?
- How many of us *feed* that failure tune that keeps playing in our heads?
- Do you have the courage to turn that tune off or switch channels to a success tune?

This situation reminds me of many successful executives today who intellectually know that they are successful, yet they have not been able to accept their success on an emotional level. I hear comments such as:

- What am I doing running this business? I have no right to be a successful vice president, entrepreneur, or general manager.
- I still see myself as the kid hustling on the basketball court.
- I come from a humble family and have worked hard, but plenty of people have helped me.

Do any of these comments sound familiar to you? Are you constantly succeeding and yet doubting yourself? Does your self-doubt sometimes cloud your judgment? What is it that continuously feeds your self-doubt?

We all have negative thoughts or occasional self-doubts. The key is not to let these overwhelm or overpower you. We all also have those little voices in our heads that give us lots of negative self-talk. The key is not to let this voice become the only voice that you hear. In the words of this successful woman, try changing or turning off the "radio station in your head" that talks about your failures.

SUCCESS EXERCISE 3: TURN OFF THE SELF-DOUBT AND TURN UP THE FACTS

To change that radio station of negative self-talk, embrace the facts of your work impact (see Chapter 4). By doing this small and powerful self-check, you are changing the voice in your head to a more fact-based and accurate account of what you can do.

For this last exercise I request that you take a minute and think about what wisdom you would want to share with your younger self. Think about when you were first starting out in your career; what were your concerns? How did you handle them in the past, and what have you learned to date that could help you move forward? If you were coaching or mentoring your younger self, what would be the biggest lesson that you would give yourself? You could think about:

- Where were you in relation to your present?
- What were your concerns?
- What were you trying to accomplish?
- What was holding you back?
- What was the one thing that pulled you forward?

Once you think in terms of your past, and then come back to the present day, you might begin to see patterns or trends in your career development. Where have you grown, where have you excelled, what is still holding you back and are you still listening to the same radio station in your head? If so, go back and review the exercises in Chapters 2 through 5 to change your radio station and get clarity on the facts of your professional impact.

What does this exercise have to do with unleashing your Inner Leader? Everything! The vast majority of these successful women tell their younger selves to break the chains that are holding them back. Overwhelmingly they tell their younger selves to believe in themselves, to believe that what they bring to the table is exceedingly valuable. They tell their younger selves to trust themselves, their instincts, their dreams, and their desires, because they are the way that they morphed into a great leader and an extraordinary person.

CASE STUDY

Jeff's publication was dedicated to education, and it was a topic that he was very passionate about. Once Jeff freed up some of his time, he began to make a plan to mentor and educate others in the topics that he believed would make a difference and allow him to live his brand of driving results through others. He had always been a good networker (see Chapter 9), and now he was getting introduced to influential people in Washington, DC, who were writing bills to introduce to the legislature. Jeff had jumped off that straight line of driving results into the Leadership Legacy cloud and was mentoring policy makers to do the right thing.

LIVING YOUR LEADERSHIP LEGACY

As you have gone through the chapters in this book, what have you discovered? Hopefully you have taken your time, done the exercises, and begun to incorporate some of the concepts in this book into your life. What is the next step?

The next step is to incorporate all that you have learned about yourself, all the productivity concepts that you have put into practice, and all the suggestions about evolving your career that you have embraced. If you have done all that, then you are on your way to *living your Leadership Legacy.*

As we followed the many case studies and sidebar stories of the people that I have coached in this book, you might have wondered what has become of some of these individuals. Are they living their Leadership Legacies, or did they just check the box, forget the learnings, and move on? I am pleased to say that many have embraced themselves and their authenticity and have, in fact, begun to live their Leadership Legacies. Following are their stories.

Finding Your Own Voice

Let's revisit Alexandra from Chapter 2. Once she held up her hand to her boss and told him that she would not take the job unless there was an increase in pay, Alexandra began to feel *authentic.* She knew deep down to her toes that for her, that was the right thing to do. By diligently being true to her strengths, she increased her awareness of the strengths that she did have. She then actively managed the times that she had to step out of her comfort zone, and she embraced *who* she authentically was to unleash her Inner Leader and lead transparently. This is the beginning of Alexandra living her Leadership Legacy.

Currently, when I speak with Alexandra, she is still happy with her life and knows that it is because she found her own voice. She figured out what makes her happy and found a working environment that fit her very well. I recently caught up with her in Washington, DC, and she was ecstatic with her life. She told me a story of how she took the bull by the horns and had a difficult conversation with a peer who had underlying misconceptions about her. Alexandra promoted herself to this person to ensure that he saw *the real Alexandra*. I smiled and toasted her and how far she had come. Her Inner Leader loves the fact that she is living her Leadership Legacy.

Following the Platinum Rule

Do you remember David from Chapter 3? David had such a strong sense of *duty* as one of his top values that he judged everyone through that lens. Because no one else was as strong in his or her beliefs as David was, he had spent the first 15 years of his career frustrated at others' seeming lack of caring. It was only when he was deeply honest with himself that he saw how much that sense of duty was hurting him and trapping his Inner Leader inside of him. Then he began to understand that other people have different values and by embracing others' values he could begin to unleash his own Inner Leader. It was his discovery of the *platinum rule* that really helped him thrive.

The platinum rule says to treat others the way that they want to be treated, not the way that you want to treat them.

Once David began to deploy the platinum rule, he became a much more effective leader. It has now been two years since my initial visit with David, and he is beginning to live his Leadership Legacy. He is still known for getting results, and he is now also known for listening to others and weighing all input before making a decision. David admitted that he actually likes living in this more authentic style, where he can shake off some of that old self-imposed sense of duty and share the responsibility with the rest of his team.

Living his Leadership Legacy has enabled David to let his Inner Leader show, and he is sleeping better at night because of it.

Sharing Impacts

In Chapter 4 we met Edward, who was simply floating along in his career. When he decided to become *serious* about his career, he started building his career currency in the form of CAR stories. Just as I had predicted to him, once he started telling his boss and others his CAR stories, they began to tell his impact to others.

The more he got comfortable with describing his impact, the more people began to see what fabulous work he had done. That also gave him the confidence to begin to tell others his strengths and values. Edward's Inner Leader was finally emerging, and he liked the positive visibility within his global organization.

Edward made a commitment to himself to become more strategic about his career evolution and joined an internal organization dedicated to helping emerging leaders. Because he had already done a lot of internal work to know himself authentically, he was the star of this group and got his next big promotion.

Edward next discovered that he was a natural mentor and began mentoring some of the individuals in his group. He had found his Leadership Legacy and made an active choice to *embrace* and *live* his Leadership Legacy. Because of his natural mentorship, he has strategically placed himself to have his next career move be to become the leader of a global product group. His Inner Leader was glad that he had stuck to his plan and done so much work to discover and live his authenticity.

Using Your Personal Brand

In Chapter 5 we met Chin, whose self-perception early on was "I am just an auditor." By going through a personal branding training program, which included many of the exercises in Part One of this book, he began to see some differentiating factors that distinguished him from his fellow partners in the firm.

Chin learned that his unique background of being born in Korea and living in both China and Japan had really made him a citizen of the world. He understood the nuances not only of each country and language but also of the international transfer tax issues associated with doing business in each of these countries. He also discovered that he was a natural networker. His strength of networking was so strong that he did not even recognize it in himself. He *loved* to connect the right people with the right resources to build incredible results.

Once Chin accepted that he brought all these brand attributes to the table, he began to act truly authentically. It was very freeing for him, especially because he is from an Asian culture, to assert to someone that *he was the one* who could help others increase his or her business in the United States. Living his Leadership Legacy became his secret weapon to not only continue to bring revenue into the firm but also live a happy and contented life with his Inner Leader shining.

Maximizing Productivity

Do you remember in Chapter 6 Tamika's reaction to the resignation of one of three team leads? It was typical; she and the other two leads would just have to work harder to take up the slack. What happened when Tamika took a step back, and with some coaching, asked her entire team to empower themselves to each take a piece of the slack? She got more help than she ever would have gotten by trying to solve the problem by herself and do so much of the work herself.

Tamika learned that being disciplined enough to delegate appropriately and successfully is a leader's secret weapon. Not only does the leader not have to shoulder the entire burden, but he or she also becomes a mentor leader to the organization by showing the trust to empower subordinates to choose their work and see it through.

That crisis of the resignation happened 10 years ago. Tamika built that organization to a pinnacle of success and has had three leadership positions since then. Just as Alexandra in Chapter 2 found her own voice, Tamika tells me that she has truly found her Inner Leader in delegating and empowering others.

Tamika is living her Leadership Legacy by being an excellent delegator and a mentor leader. She thrives in an environment of driving results through empowering and mentoring the people in her organization. By living her Leadership Legacy, she has become known in health care circles and has recently been asked to be on the board of directors of a hospital and health care association. Tamika's Inner Leader is doing what she loves to do and what she has discovered she is good at.

Mentoring Others

Mentoring is a fabulous way to live your Leadership Legacy. I have worked with more than 4,000 clients and have guided probably half of them through the process of finding and working with a mentor. In all those numbers of people, fewer than potentially 10 mentors have not agreed to mentor that person right now. To me, that is amazing. While there might not be anyone in your organization whose job it is to evolve your career for you, there are hundreds of people out there who would be happy to be your mentor.

Melanie from Chapter 7 was my second client when I started my coaching firm more than a decade ago. Since she went to work for Jan, she has moved into six positions in three companies and is currently a vice president of a 200-person division in a global health care company. The one lesson that Jan taught her that she will never forget is always to be open to having a mentoring relationship with others. Melanie lives her Leadership Legacy by mentoring others.

I have mentioned that I have been involved with the Healthcare Businesswomen's Association (HBA) for 10 years now. Eight years ago some very strategic women started a formal mentoring program. I have been a part of it since the beginning and it has been very successful. The key to their success is a detailed survey that both the mentors and the mentees fill out so that the groups are well matched. They keep people who work at the same company in separate groups, they match goals of mentees to mentors with that experience, and they even match on logistics (for example, whether someone can meet only at lunch or after work).

Being part of this program has been tremendously rewarding for me. The first reason is because I was matched with women whom I would never have known otherwise. This appeals to my strengths of being a relator, a communicator, and a connector. Second, lest you think that these meetings are just a chat session, the results that my mentees have had encourage my achiever and maximizer with such a sense of satisfaction. Most of the groups are two mentors and four mentees. Each year for the past eight years, the majority of my mentees have made a job or level change during the nine months that they were in my mentoring group. Third, I have had a few mentees become good friends who consistently have my back and give me heartfelt smiles. Living that Leadership Legacy makes my Inner Leader contented and happy.

Anyone can enter into a mentoring relationship and live his or her Leadership Legacy reaping the rewards of this behavior—*what are you waiting for?*

Using Effective Personal Language

In Chapter 8 we met Howard, who already was a visionary leader. He had the natural achievement strength, liked to work on significant projects, and was in the formal position of the lead partner in his firm. He felt very comfortable in a position of command, seeing the future vision and making decisions on how to get there.

But Howard's Inner Leader was not smiling. He was very frustrated because he somehow could not convince the people around him to follow him in a manner that made both him and his organization comfortable.

Howard took the courageous step to understand what *he* could do to have his Inner Leader emerge and propel his organization to the place where it would maximize profits. Making a change in one's communication style is one of the hardest changes to make, and Howard's perseverance paid off.

Howard is now living his Leadership Legacy by being the leader who he was born to be. The people in his organization feel *heard;* they *know* that Howard listens to them. They also know that Howard will ask the difficult questions for everyone to get the facts and make the correct decision based on accurate input. It took Howard almost two years to change his personal communication style completely and be comfortable with the change. His firm is prospering and his earlier emotional reactions are waning. He is living his Leadership Legacy and is proud that his authentic Inner Leader finally emerged.

Evolving Your Career

In Chapter 9 we met many professionals who finally took the plunge to take control of evolving their careers. Do you remember Rachel, who turned a seemingly bad situation of losing her job into a lifelong learning experience of networking to keep her career evolving? Whenever Rachel asks me to get together, I get excited because I know that she has another new project in mind, by which she is giving back to other professionals. She puts the fun in giving back to others.

As mentioned in Chapter 9, Rachel started the Women's Reinvent Yourself Series at her company and then was invited to take it to a larger venue. Her next project was to develop a program called Social Circles. For the pilot program, she had an application process, three women were chosen, and they met with Rachel; I volunteered as the mentor coach. Rachel then found three key executives who agreed to meet with each of the participants to give her advice about evolving her career. After meeting for six months, each woman got a substantial promotion and her Inner Leader was smiling.

Rachel's Leadership Legacy did not stop there. Each of these women in the pilot then decided to start her own Social Circle. Now these women are living *their* Leadership Legacy.

In summary, unleashing your Inner Leader to ultimately live your Leadership Legacy starts slow and small. People must understand themselves, then uncover their personal strengths, values, impact, and personal brand. Once you feel comfortable with yourself, then you can take the leap to improve productivity, mentor others, cultivate leadership language, and evolve your career.

It is at this point that people look backward to realize that past successes are leading them to a future path of living their Leadership Legacy. If that path is not a direction that you want to go, then lose the fear, get a buddy to help you, and take your first step to the new road that will eventually lead you in the direction of living your Leadership Legacy.

If those past success are exactly right for you, then embrace them, and take larger leaps to realize and live your Leadership Legacy fully.

CAREER EVOLUTION: BUILDING YOUR LEADERSHIP LEGACY CHAPTER SUMMARY

- Your Leadership Legacy is not in the past; rather the idea is to live it now and in the future.

- Understanding what makes you happy and fulfilled is the first step to building your Leadership Legacy.

- Success Exercise 1: What will success look like? For every project that you are involved in, ask, "What does success look like for this project?" Then ask, "What does success look like for me? What about this situation will fulfill me?"

- Success Exercise 2: Uncover your subconscious. Buy a bound book and make a commitment to journal three pages every day for three weeks. Then review what you have written to find what is hidden that is holding you back.

- Success Exercise 3: Turn off the self-doubt and turn up the facts. What wisdom would you like to share with your younger self? What can you do now to take the advice that you would share with your younger self?

Examples from case studies in previous chapters of my coaching clients living their Leadership Legacy

- Alexandra in Chapter 2 *found her own voice* and actively managed the times that she had to step out of her comfort zone to embrace who she was authentically. She now leads in a transparent manner and is living her Leadership Legacy.

- David's sense of duty in Chapter 3 was holding him back from effective leadership. Once he began to deploy the platinum rule of treating others the way that they want to be treated, he became a much more effective leader.

- Edward discovered that he was a natural mentor in Chapter 4. He made the active choice to embrace and live his Leadership Legacy. This has placed him in a career evolution to the next position as the leader of a global team.

- Chin was amazed at his self-discoveries in Chapter 5. His natural ability to network across cultural boundaries freed him to achieve while doing what he loved to do and bringing in revenue to the firm.

- Tamika's team lead's resignation 10 years ago helped her build her Leadership Legacy in Chapter 6. Discovering her strengths of delegation and mentorship has enabled her to continue to produce results with a more empowered team.

- Melanie in Chapter 7 overcame her fear of asking people to mentor her, and that has been her secret weapon that has catapulted her career to where she is today. She loves living her Leadership Legacy.

- Howard's frustrated Inner Leader in Chapter 8 took the courageous step to understand what *he* could do to have his Inner Leader emerge and propel his organization to the place where it would maximize profits. Making a change in one's communication style is one of the hardest changes to make and Howard's perseverance paid off.

- Rachel in Chapter 9 turned a seemingly bad situation of losing her job into a lifelong learning experience of networking to keep her career evolving. By learning to help others evolve their careers, Rachel has also learned the lesson of making giving back fun.

- Jeff in this chapter will always touch a soft spot in my heart. He was already so successful and the self-discovery of what his personal brand was and how it fit into his evolving his Leadership Legacy makes my Inner Leader smile.

PART
THREE

Inspire Your Inner Leader

As you have traveled this leadership journey in this book, the hope is that you have gotten inspiration from the case studies and coaching stories associated with each chapter. These examples were meant to augment your understanding of the techniques and concepts being discussed.

Part Three presents another type of inspiration.

I sent a request to my community for their inspiration. The invitation was to share what moment in time, personal encounter, saying, or quotation gave them the inspiration that they needed then. I am honored and grateful that so many took the time to share their personal insights and tales.

The following pages tell their stories. There is a lot in each of these chapters. You might want to read them all at once, or you might want to take it in small bites, perhaps whenever you need a dose of inspiration from one of the chapters. Take your time, read them, think about the concepts, and then reread them. Once you have become familiar with what is in each chapter, you can also save it for those special moments when you need to hear of a success story, or potentially refer to these stories when you need to encourage a friend or colleague in one of these categories.

The fun thing about inspiration is that it can inspire many times over. I sincerely hope that these chapters give you the encouragement when you need it most and that you find some favorite stories that you turn to often.

CHAPTER 11

Guiding Principles

Your journey of unleashing your Inner Leader will help you find inspiration. Inspiration comes in many forms and the most powerful is in the form of a story. The inspirational stories are divided into four chapters, the first of which is "Guiding Principles."

One guiding principle is to live with intention. "If you want to go far, go together" is the guiding principle that says that team is the most important element of success. Understanding people and building relationships by leveraging your strengths is a guiding principle.

Sometimes, what got you to your current success will not get you to future success. Taking small steps to move you toward your goal is what helps give you the courage to keep going. Making a failure and learning from it can lead to success.

Procrastination of decision making means that you can miss out on life's opportunities. Conversely, hitting the pause button to make sure that your decisions align with your values is a guiding principle. Inspirational quotes from famous people can be the words to remind you of your guiding principle. Being true to your values and never selling out is the way to make the right decision.

As you continue your journey of unleashing your Inner Leader, you will, no doubt, find inspiration along the way. Inspiration can come in many forms. For me, my leadership inspiration comes not only from books and quotes but also from an unexpected moment or interaction and, most important, from other people's stories.

Rather than sharing only what inspires me, I asked my community to share what inspires them. I received a large number of responses, which told me that inspiration was important to all. These inspirational messages came in many ways, and the single thread that ran through all was a *story*. Even when the initial inspiration was a quote or a saying, it was important to that individual because it was part of a personal story for him or her. The *story* of the circumstances of when he or she first heard the saying or when the quote became a guiding principle that the person used as a leadership beacon or a guiding light was the important piece.

GUIDING PRINCIPLES

As we learned in Chapter 3, your personal values are the rock that you stand on. When your environment aligns with your values, you will behave in the most authentic manner possible and your Inner Leader will emerge. The first chapter of inspirational stories contains experiences from individuals who have learned the lesson of using their personal values as a guiding principle. Some tell the story of a struggle when things just did not seem right and eventually they realized that it was because their values were being violated. They then had to find a way to make things right and get back in sync with their values. Enjoy the inspirations below and hopefully you will resonate with many of these individuals, their situations, and what got them through. As you read these stories, please remember that:

- Your values are the rock that you stand on.
- When your values align with your environment, you will behave in your most authentic manner and your Inner Leader can emerge. The opposite is true; when your values do not align with your environment, you will feel unnerved, out of sorts, emotional, or simply depressed.
- The benefit to understanding and living your values is that you get clarity and a positive return on your expenditure of emotional energy.
- If something does not feel right, it is probably because it violates your values.

● The following are stories in which the person finds inspiration and then relates how this actually became a guiding principle in his or her life.

A network consulting engineer with a marketing background working for a global software company sent the following:

PROFILE

▼ I have two things to share: a quote and a saying.

The quote that I come back to most often is "*Live with intention.*" I think it's easy to become caught up in other people's plans or to just coast through our routines and go through the motions. When I find myself in a rut or getting stressed, I remind myself of this quote because it helps to center me and bring me back to what's important. I can then realign and refresh my perspective to make sure I stay on track to doing and becoming what I want.

This saying came from a drink bottle cap:

> If you want to go quickly, go alone; if you want to go far, go together.
> — *African proverb*

I find this one to be so powerful because people often think their journey to the top must be done alone or at the expense of those around them. If everyone realized we could all go so much further through cooperation and support, I think the world would be a better place.

This person's guiding principle is all about being intentional in actions and collaborative in work. Having a clear goal for your behavior and your work gives clarity to unleashing your Inner Leader and living your Leadership Legacy.

The next story is from a project manager working for a global clinical trials company (also called a contract research organization CRO). When she came to our coaching engagement, she was having a difficult time with her manager. Discovering her strengths (see Chapter 2) was an exciting realization for her. Understanding herself through her strengths gave her a baseline from which to view her manager—especially what worked and what did not work between them. We both were thrilled that she reached such inspirational heights.

PROFILE

I have a passion for understanding people and building relationships. This passion gained momentum after enduring a difficult relationship with my manager who compromised my personal development and damaged my spirit due to her own insecurities. I allowed her to have this detrimental impact on me. I know now this challenging relationship was actually the opportunity for me to *Live by the 3 L's: Let it go. Learn from it. Launch change.* This is a great quote featured in Woman's Advantage Wisdom calendar by Michelle Hill (http://womansadvantage.biz/products/the-woman-s-advantage-shared-wisdom-calendar) and it has a home taped to my computer as a constant reminder. By taking the time to connect with people, challenging or not, I listen and learn, build trust, effectively problem solve and create solutions. This commitment to people aligns perfectly with my strengths (from *StrengthsFinder 2.0*) of being a relator, learner, achiever, restorative and responsible. Clearly this is my innate calling as I mentor more people in the benefits of cultivating human to human connections.

As I grow older I want to share my "opportunity" wisdom with my children (two daughters aged 9 and 7) so they know at young ages how to best care for their surrounding community. While our children are our future, our future is brighter if we can find a way to perform better by getting along. I often remind them to *Finish Strong* (my personal motto) in anything they tackle and that they can only control themselves. If others are unkind or lie, they must always be honest and make the right choices. That is our guiding principle: walking with integrity that will impact how others treat you.

A few weeks ago, I volunteered for the Special Olympics—undoubtedly a life changing experience. Yesterday, my oldest daughter informed me that she made a request to her elementary school to connect students with those whom are more challenged mentally and/or physically as a way to unite all students and have an appreciation for all kinds of people. The proud mother in me held back an honored tear, while my motivation increased, knowing how powerful the trickling effect of building relationships is.

Bottom line, there is a leader in each of us. It starts with building relationships which are key to our emotions, engagement, and performance. That is my inspiration!

It was such a joy to be a coaching partner with this person, to help her uncover her guiding principle of living in accord with her strengths. There is lot in the above story. The first element is taking a bad situation with a manager who had all but beaten down this person's self-confidence and turning it into a quest to find a guiding principle by which to live by. The second element is embracing the concept of living in accord with your strengths and building relationships will ensure a strong future. Third is the idea of modeling your behavior so that others follow, whether it is a friend, a work colleague, or your own child!

Seth Godin has an interesting take on a guiding principle (*Seth's Blog*, "What Got You Here ... " http://ow.ly/xnTJQ). As discussed in Chapter 10, many times when asked about unleashing your Inner Leader to build your Leadership Legacy, I remind my clients that what got you here is not going to get you there (where you want to go next). It is our personal responsibility to constantly monitor our Inner Leader and make sure that we are keeping it current with our evolving environment and inner authenticity. I share Godin's post because I believe that he says it well.

 What Got You Here ...

PROFILE

Without a doubt, your hard work in test prep led to better SAT (Scholastic Aptitude Test) scores, which got you into college. It's not clear, though, that SAT prep skills are going to help you ever again.

I know that all those years of practicing (8 hours a day!) got you plenty of praise and allowed you to reach a high level on the bassoon. It's not clear, though, that practicing even more is going to be the thing that takes your career where you want it to go.

Of course you needed a very special set of skills to raise all that money for your company. But now, you've raised it. Those same skills aren't what you need to actually build your company into something that matters, though.

Successful people develop a winning strategy. It's the work and focus and tactics that they get rewarded for, the stuff they do that others often don't, and it works—until it doesn't.

When times get confusing, it's easy to revert to the habits that got you here. More often than not, that's precisely the wrong approach. The very thing that got you here is the thing that everyone who's here is doing, and if that's what it took to get to the next level, no one would be stuck.

I am a big fan of Godin, and I believe that this blog excerpt has a huge message about discovering and living by your guiding principle. Remember Jeff in Chapter 10? He was very successful, but continuing to drive results was not going to get him to where he wanted to go. He wanted to still drive results *and* be a mentor leader to the great team that he had built. Remember his brand statement, "Driving results through compassionate leadership." It took some changes in his behavior and actions to embrace this guiding principle and be inspirational to others. Jeff is an example of what Godin is saying in this blog excerpt—what got you to the place of success is not what will get you further; deciding what your Leadership Legacy is and how you want to live your Legacy is the next step.

A financial industry business enablement manager sent this piece of inspiration:

PROFILE

I came across this quote on Facebook the other day that spoke to me:

> Courage is not having the strength to go on, it is going on when you don't have the strength.

In the past couple of years, I've gone through some major changes in my life. During the difficult times, I had absolutely no idea how I was going to live through it all. I felt like I had no more strength or fight left in me to get through yet another day. With the support of family, friends, and faith in God, I managed to come through. I never thought of myself as a courageous person. But remembering those dark and cold winter nights when I walked back to the car alone after visiting my daughter in the hospital … moving across the country by myself … and never losing faith. I realized that … I AM a courageous person because I fought on when I did not have the strength!

Courage is such an interesting word, and after living through some dark times, the word *courage* has recently become this person's guiding principle. In Chapter 6 we learned of the concept of your secret advantage, which means making a decision to take action, regardless of how small, when you really do not have the energy to do it, consistently, will ultimately catapult you forward. In his book *One Small Step Can Change Your Life: The Kaizen Way,* Robert Maurer (Workman, 2004) espouses the same technique.

This person lived by her values and did not even realize it until her crisis was over. That is when she discovered that pulling on your inner courage is an inspiring guiding principle.

I met a former IBM technical project director when he had been laid off during the economic dip of 2008–2009. He struggled for a few years trying to identify his strengths, values, and personal brand and what his version of success was rather than what others have always suggested to him. Although he did lots of looking and interviewing, no position truly seemed right for him. In his networking efforts he discovered a Chinese networking group that was dedicated to attracting Chinese business to the North Carolina Research Triangle area. Being a Chinese American, he finally felt like he was *home* and became the executive director of this group. Below is what he sent as his guiding principle:

PROFILE

I have enjoyed reading your newsletters every month for the last five years. As you prepare your book I am glad that you will be able to help others as you have helped me.

My suggested quote would be: "*Failures are the mother of success.*"

I can testify to that quote because I had gone through a long journey of 2.5 years of looking for employment. You helped me overcome the many failed interviews and motivated me to keep looking for that perfect match. I also remember that one of the high technique industry icons, Steve Jobs, had failed many times in his life. But ultimately in the past 10 years of his life, his visions of creating the innovative products that change the way we live was realized. Those innovations were the accumulation of many failed experiences. John C. Maxwell also has a book talking about this topic that is called *Failing Forward: Turning Mistakes into Stepping Stones for Success* (Thomas Nelson, 2007).

I have had many failures and without them, I would never have gotten to my present position of working in an area that I am passionate about. I hope this "*Failures are the mother of success*" concept will be useful for your book and helpful for your readers.

It is an honor to hear that my newsletters have inspired people. There have been many months that writing a newsletter was the last thing that I wanted to do, and hearing stories like this one always inspires me to continue and do what I need to do. My work as a coach puts me in situations where I experience the dedication and effort of my clients as they push themselves to move forward. Many coaching engagements are inspiring to me, and I feel the need to share them with my community. This was a special inspiration for me because he finally found his place by living and embracing his failures. The idea of embracing failure as a guiding principle has propelled many people forward.

A saying from a grandmother was the inspiration behind this business manager in the financial planning and analysis division of a global software firm. He is known for being a decisive manager and legacy leader.

PROFILE

This quote comes from my 94-year-old grandmother.

Some people are procrastinators of life and then miss out on life from not being able to make a decision.

I have lived by this principle since I started my first job after finishing college.

What wisdom and what a powerful guiding principle! Combining the idea of making decisions so that one does not miss out on life with the previous story of embracing failures could make a person unstoppable. Making an educated decision, then learning and living with the outcome, was this person's inspiration from a very early age.

One of the most satisfying times in my career was being a part of Healthcare Businesswomen's Association's (HBA) mentoring program since its inception seven years ago. This next piece of inspirational advice comes from one of my co-mentors in the form of her biggest tip and biggest piece of advice. If after reading this you want to think more about your values, please go back to Chapter 3 and complete the exercises in that chapter.

▼ Biggest tip: *Press the pause button.* Many people "breathe," but for me I needed something more "visual" and this button idea is helpful. While pressing the button, think about the big picture, think about the other person's perspective, think of how you can ask a question and avoid statements (statements are positional). Worst case, buy yourself some time by saying a phrase such as "Can we come back to this?" or "I would like to take the time this deserves to consider all things/more things" or "Let's take this off line." Any statement that allows you to pause and take that needed breath is what you are looking to get here.

Biggest advice: *Never sell yourself out. Be true to your values.* If the company is not going in a direction that you believe honors your values or honors the mission they stand for, then do your best to influence change … don't accept status quo—leaders don't accept status quo (but it doesn't always make them popular). If that doesn't work, look for something else that fulfills you that aligns with your values. TRUST that standing up for your true values is a worthwhile investment in you; even if the rest of the world thinks you are crazy. Bottom line, none of us are promised tomorrow, so why waste today investing in something you don't believe in?

Thank you to my former co-mentor for this insight. Interesting how her inspiration is to hit the pause button before making a decision. She obviously has learned from her failures and has determined that for her, the best outcomes come from hitting the pause button and taking into account her values before making a decision. Her life goal is to live her Leadership Legacy by being true to her values and making sure that her decisions consider this.

Two women whom I have known for the past six years are the ultimate volunteers. Although they both have day jobs, their heart is in helping others improve. They have both co-chaired the Connected Women of North Carolina group. When I sent out the request for inspirational stories, they wrote back that they had just finished writing a newsletter, and with their permission I have added it below. A note: while this was written for a women's group, I have more and more male clients who are feeling the pain of balancing work and family life. Making career decisions has become increasingly more complex because these fathers, husbands, and sons want to have the flexibility to spend more time with those whom they love.

PROFILE

Confession: We love being professional working mothers/fathers; it's an incredible experience ... but it isn't always easy. An adventure? Definitely. All sunshine and rainbows? *Not so much.*

So where do you turn when you're feeling the weight of the world on your shoulders? When you need some sort of a motivational pick-me-up? For us, quotes are the key.

Quotes serve as a quick reminder that we're not alone in this, that others have been where we are, that there is a light at the end of the tunnel, and that anything and everything is possible. They help to spark our brilliance, inspire creativity, and turbo-boost us into "get it done" mode.

Now, there are a lot of great quotes out there; so we've scoured the Web to find the quotes that we feel are the best ones to inspire, empower, and motivate us to greatness.

> Don't limit yourself. Many people limit themselves to what they think they can do. You can go as far as your mind lets you. What you believe, remember, you can achieve.
> — Mary Kay Ash, founder, Mary Kay Cosmetics

> My philosophy is that not only are you responsible for your life, but doing the best at this moment puts you in the best place for the next moment.
> — Oprah Winfrey, American television host, actress, producer, and philanthropist

> When one door of happiness closes, another opens; but often we look so long at the closed door that we do not see the one which has opened for us.
> — Helen Keller, author, political activist, and speaker

> Most of us have trouble juggling. The woman who says she doesn't is someone whom I admire but have never met.
> — Barbara Walters, broadcast journalist and author

> Begin doing what you want to do now. We are not living in eternity. We have only this moment, sparkling like a star in our hand—and melting like a snowflake.
> — Marie Beyon Ray, author

> You gain strength, courage and confidence by every
> experience in which you really stop to look fear in the face.
> You are able to say to yourself, 'I lived through this horror.
> I can take the next thing that comes along.' You must do the
> thing you think you cannot do.
> — Eleanor Roosevelt, former first lady

I thank these two ultimate volunteers because it seems like the quotes that they picked do reflect the concepts that I touted in Chapter 10. That is, you are limitless. You can go as far as your dreams, aspirations, and hard work will take you.

It is nice that others look to these famous people as inspiration to keep moving forward. Thank you to my community for your submissions.

Have you found some inspiration in the above stories? What have they inspired you to do? If you were lacking hope, did they give you some? If you were struggling with a problem, did they tear the shroud from your eyes and give you a clear vision? If you are already successful and happy, did they inspire you to do more, to strive to move yourself to a greater place of authenticity?

If you have been inspired and have a story to share, please send it to CoachVickie10@gmail.com and then you might be the one who will inspire others.

GUIDING PRINCIPLES CHAPTER SUMMARY

- Your journey of unleashing your Inner Leader will help you find inspiration. Inspiration comes in many forms and the most powerful is in the form of a story.
- One guiding principle is to live with intention.
- If you want to go far, team is the most important element of success.
- Understanding people and building relationships by leveraging your strengths is a guiding principle.

- Sometimes, what got you to your current success will not get you to future success.

- Taking small steps to move you toward your goal is what helps give you the courage to keep going.

- Making a failure and learning from it can lead to success.

- Procrastination on decision making means that you can miss out on life's opportunities.

- Conversely, hitting the pause button to make sure that your decisions align with your values is a guiding principle.

- Being true to your values and never selling out is the way to make the right decision.

- Inspirational quotes from famous people can be the words to remind you of your guiding principle.

CHAPTER **12**

Letting Go of *Me* to Get to *Us*

I n this chapter we will read inspirational stories about letting go of yourself and focusing on your teams. Unleashing your Inner Leader means letting go of yourself and focusing your efforts on the team with whom you are working. A good leader asks his or her people to seek alternatives rather than simply giving them the answer.

When a leader removes distractions, the team can have a clear path to become experts. This builds confidence among the team, which then develops into trust and respect. A good leader listens to his or her people, keeps his or her eye on the basics, and clears the road so that the team has a clear path to success. A leader is best when people fail to know that he or she exists.

Success happens when leaders make the commitment to push themselves out of the way and give their people the room to do it themselves.

Much of discovering your Inner Leader is based on understanding yourself, as we discovered in Part One of this book. Once that journey helps you realize your authentic self, the second part of unleashing your Inner Leader is to put all those self-discoveries to work.

LETTING GO OF *ME* TO GET TO *US*

In this chapter we will become inspired by people who discovered that unleashing their Inner Leader really meant letting go of themselves and focusing on the team with whom they were working. As we saw throughout Part Two and especially in Chapter 6 when discussing delegation, one of the hardest tasks for a leader to accomplish is to let go. In the following inspirational stories we will learn how others conquered this task and let their Leadership Legacy begin to form.

The first inspirational story is from a 20-year veteran software programmer and a fellow golf partner. She talks about a lesson that she learned early in her career, which has provided inspiration many times over.

PROFILE

About six months into my first job out of school, I was assigned a task and got to a point where I didn't know how to proceed. I went to my mentor and asked him what to do. He asked me what my suggestions were. I didn't have any—any good ones at least. He told me to go away and don't come back until I had three alternatives and a recommendation. At the time, I couldn't believe he wasn't giving me the answer and pushed back. He repeated … go away and don't come back without three alternatives. I did and later went back with three proposals and the supporting rationale of which one I thought was best. We then had a constructive conversation and we went with my best suggestion.

What this taught me was that in business, unlike in school, the leaders don't always have the answers. They expect you to think and since you're closer to the issue, come up with alternatives. Then they're able to talk through these with you and help you come to the best joint decision.

As I became a team lead, I have told this story hundreds of times as I make the same request of my team. Some people call it empowerment; I simply call it common sense.

Because I have always known this person only as my golf buddy, I was honored that she thought my book project was worthy of her words. I was also inspired by her story; leaders do not always need to have the answers. This was exactly the lesson that Tamika learned in Chapter 6, to ask more questions and empower your team to find the answers. In Chapter 8 I presented exercises of asking *what* questions. Out of context, this might not seem very conversational. However, once you master the technique, it is very useful for opening up the space for an individual to realize that there are alternatives. Whether you call that empowering or simply common sense—it works!

The next inspirational story has a similar lesson with a strong emotional twist. As a friend of a friend whom I met 17 years ago, we got to know each other when he asked for my professional help in a career transition situation. In the manufacturing industry and the quality functional area, his leadership talents skyrocketed when he decided to let go.

PROFILE

As a leader for a team of 11 quality engineers, I get my inspiration by helping them to succeed in their deliverables. My philosophy is to remove as many distractions as possible so they have a clear path to focus on the expected functionality of the application they are testing. I focus on helping them be the experts of their domain. This builds confidence and confidence builds trust with their project team peers. Once trust is on the team, respect follows. When a team, both the project team and functional team, has confidence and respect, doors will open to bring the team to higher levels of satisfaction and personal growth. When my team grows, so do I.

What an unselfish view of letting your Inner Leader shine through. As was discussed in Chapter 6, this leader removed distractions to empower his team to drive deliverables. He wants to build his team into a group of experts. Once obstacles are removed, the team can function at high efficiency. This type of environment can then build some strong emotional ties of trust and respect. The following emotions of trust and respect ensure that his team is being led by someone who is living his Leadership Legacy.

In a similar vein, this director of the donor program for the philanthropic arm of a global financial professional services firm has learned a huge lesson from one of his favorite books.

I love and often reflect on some of the items listed in "12 Things Good Bosses Believe" from Robert I. Sutton, professor of science and engineering at Stanford. (See http://bobsutton.typepad.com/.) They help serve as a compass and a measuring stick for my work most days. Here are a few of my favorites.

"2. My success—and that of my people—depends largely on being the master of obvious and mundane things, not on magical, obscure, or breakthrough ideas or methods."

I love this because it says to me—keep your eye on the basics so your people reach higher.

"7. I aim to fight as if I am right, and listen as if I am wrong—and to teach my people to do the same thing."

I always try to drive for results but be human. The best way to do that is to listen to your people!

"10. Bad is stronger than good. It's more important to eliminate the negative than to accentuate the positive."

This tells me that a good leader helps create momentum by clearing the road!

This inspirational submission once again signals that if leaders can put their ego aside and truly believe in their team, then amazing things can happen. I was particularly struck by the statement, "Bad is stronger than good." This person's goal is to eliminate the negative and create momentum by clearing the road. It also reminds me that when you are tempted to go for the *me* and forget the *we,* you are falling into the category of not clearing the road. Remember that everyone has an Inner Leader inside of him or her. As we have seen in the previous stories, one of the ways to unleash that Inner Leader is to think about removing obstacles and clearing the way for your team to think about alternatives.

Another inspiration comes from someone with a PhD in molecular biology who got her start at Johnson & Johnson and has been evolving her leadership competencies throughout her entire career. After leaving Johnson & Johnson she ran a successful consulting practice for a decade and has been lured back to a big pharmaceutical company, where she is leading a successful global development team. Her big leadership lessons took place when she learned to give up her existence for the success of her team. She shares her knowledge in two quotes.

PROFILE

People become really quite remarkable when they start thinking they can do things.
— *Norman Vincent Peale*

One of the first tasks of a leader is to build a team. In business, we cannot always pick the members of that team yet we must find a way to work as an effective force. The magic occurs when individuals come together around a shared goal and see themselves as an important and integral part of reaching it. It's hard to stop a group with a common vision who believes that it can achieve an outcome that will make a difference.

A leader is best when people barely know he exists, not so good when people obey and acclaim him. Worse when they despise him. Fail to honor people, they fail to honor you.
— *Lao Tzu*

It's easy for individuals in senior positions to assume that they are the key to the success of the organization and take credit for achievements. The truly excellent leaders know that it's the people who make the success happen and express the fact that it was the combined efforts of all of them that made the difference.

I worked with this woman in a volunteer capacity and she does live this inspiration. She truly honors the people on her team. In StrengthsFinder language (see Chapter 2), her top strength is *individualization;* this means that she literally sees people for who they are and she actually does *honor* who they are. I witnessed her establish a formal all-volunteer mentor program. Her success came from providing an inspiring common goal and then building an environment in which each individual felt secure enough to mentor his or her way (within a certain structure). Then, when someone wanted to do it outside of the set structure, this leader made some modifications and enabled her to proceed. She has discovered and is living her Leadership Legacy.

The next inspiration is from a good friend of many years. Her background is as an art major who ended up at a technology gaming company as the director of art and science operations. She and her team build the sets and do the shoots for video game production. She has discovered that when you give up yourself and clear the path for your team to produce, it is a whole lot of fun!

PROFILE

I used to be a "doer," thinking that I had to do everything myself to get satisfaction. I hired people to help, but because I feared they might fail if given the opportunity, I refrained from letting them try things at first.

Then, one day, I stepped outside that and let one of them do it—I mean, really let them do it. Sure, it wasn't exactly like I would have done, but hey, it was good. And, in fact, as I did this more often, I realized they actually had some pretty good ideas when given the chance. They blossomed and grew. It was like watching a rose bud become a full-on rose!

Now, I rarely *do* things, but instead, I use my creativity to inspire my staff to do things—to continue to grow and bloom. Today, I get great satisfaction out of inspiring them to do well—to take the lead. And I stay out of it. I find myself being more of a traffic cop/cheerleader in my leadership role. And that's a whole lot of fun.

This is another beautiful example of letting go of you to move the team to where it can ultimately be. Note that for this person it was hard to let go, and she had to force herself not to step in. This idea of forcing yourself to empower your people not only is hard but also sometimes takes longer to let someone else do it and to mentor him or her through it. Yes, in today's time-sensitive world that is a worry, and yet when we make the commitment to ourselves to take the time and remove obstacles, great things happen. Are you beginning to see how to unleash your Inner Leader and empower your team to take the lead and shine?

Have these stories above inspired you? Have they given you the motivation to get out of your team's way and let it discover its own Inner Leader? Do you think that you can let go of *me* to get your group to *us*? Have you been convinced of the value of stepping away and asking your people for their suggestions? Are you ready to have fun as a leader?

All these leaders have learned the secret of letting go, and I encourage you to do the same. Go back over Chapters 6, 7, and 8 in Part Two; review the exercises about delegation, asking *what* questions, your personal language, and being a mentor. Your Inner Leader will be smiling.

If you have been inspired and have a story to share, please send it to CoachVickie10@gmail.com and then you might be the one who will inspire others.

LETTING GO OF *ME* TO GET TO *US* CHAPTER SUMMARY

- Unleashing your Inner Leader means letting go of yourself and focusing on the team with whom you are working.
- A good leader asks his or her people to seek alternatives rather than simply giving them the answer.
- When a leader removes distractions, the team can have a clear path to become experts. This builds confidence among the team, which then develops into trust and respect.
- A good leader listens to his or her people, keeps his or her eye on the basics, and clears the road so that the team has a clear path to success.
- A leader is best when people fail to know that he or she exists.
- Success happens when leaders make the commitment to push themselves out of the way and give their people the room to do it themselves.

CHAPTER 13

Reflecting on the Past to Get to the Future

Stopping and hitting the pause button for reflection is essential for each of us to unleash our Inner Leader and ensure that we are going in the right direction. Reflection before projection ensures that past successes are understood and celebrated. Then the learnings of the reflection are incorporated into the projections of the future.

Reflection can happen when a person is forced into a situation such as a job loss or a serious illness. That is when all the insights learned in Part One of this book become increasingly important to use when projecting the future. Sometimes after reflection, fear of failure gets in the way of projection. Taking the view of failure being a road to success is a way of unleashing your Inner Leader. A successful leader reflects so that the conversation can then be directed to how that success gives the team the experience and insights to tackle the next big project.

REFLECTING ON THE PAST TO GET TO THE FUTURE

One of the concerns that I have when working with very successful leaders is that they do not build into their busy schedules enough time for reflecting. I know that we are all so busy that it is hard to find time for many things that we want to do, and time for reflection should be on the top of the list.

The technique that I sometimes suggest is simply to make a list of 5 to 10 questions to ask yourself when you decide to take some pause time. Maybe you could have a quiet lunch alone and reflect on a particular subject. In Chapter 10, I shared a list of questions that I asked Jeff at the beginning of our coaching engagement. In that same chapter is an exercise about asking yourself questions to help define what success is for you. No matter what the subject, taking time for reflection, whether in the form of questions or not, is a key for future success.

Stopping and hitting the pause button for reflection is essential for each of us to unleash our Inner Leader and ensure that we are going in the right direction.

Reflecting on the past before rushing to the future has become a constant theme for me, especially around the New Year. Each year we rush to close up projects and measure end-of-the-year results. Then we rush headfirst into the New Year with all kinds of planning activities and ready-to-implement goals. To start this section, I have reproduced a newsletter that I wrote in December 2009 about reflection before projection.

 December 2009: Reflection before Projection

Healthcare Businesswomen's Association (HBA) is one of my favorite organizations because there is always an array of smart, degreed women who are serious about their career advancement and about helping others succeed as well. At our recent holiday meeting I had a conversation about leaders doing more reflection. When socializing the concept with some of the attendees, what struck me was the comment made by the owner of a small medical writing business, "*Wow*, Vickie, reflection before projection, what a great way to start the New Year!" Thank you, Robin, I appreciate your phrase. I believe that this is something that many of us are not doing and it is essential for long-term success!

How many times do we naturally transition from the holiday break into January with all of our sights set full steam ahead on the next year's goals and performance indicators? Do we ever actually spend enough time reflecting on the past year and assessing our performance? Even more important, how much time do we actually spend reviewing our successes and reveling in the fact that we overcame some intense odds to finish the year strong? The follow-on question is: How much time do we actually spend celebrating those successes and showing sincere appreciation to our teams for all the hard work, personal sacrifice, and effective solutions? Most important, do we celebrate or show our appreciation to those outside our business (*way* inside of our lives—family, spouses, and friends) for their unending support of our long working hours, missed personal events, and occasional grumpy moods?

If any of this rings true for you, I ask that before you continue to think about next year's planning, forecasting, and projections, please stop, thoughtfully reflect, and then take some action:

- Take a survey of your group's thoughts, attitudes, and desires relating to last year's performance and share the results with your team and manager.

- Write a personal note to those top team members and their families thanking them for a job well done and explaining in a personal manner what it means to you to have them on your team (see Chapter 9).

- Bring your group together for a group assessment of their past year's performance. Ask each person to bring their top success for the year written in the Challenge, Action, Result (CAR) format (see Chapter 4).

- Schedule some quiet time and reflect on all of the successes that you have personally driven in the last year and make plans to celebrate.

- Make an appointment with your manager with the sole purpose of reflecting on last year's results; again, present them in the CAR format.

- Send a gift basket to your family as a thank you for their support.

- Tell your family as a group what their support has meant to you.

- *Stop* giving compliments followed with a *but* (see Chapter 8).

While these suggestions might seem frivolous or elementary, the message is very bottom line–oriented. You cannot accurately project next year's successes without taking a good, hard look at what happened this year. Congratulations, you are on your way to making the best New Year's plan that you have ever created by completing some "reflection before projection" and *deriving results from within*.

I am a strong believer in reflection. In today's fast-paced world we sometimes jump from one thing to another and do not hit that pause button. The story of Martha in Chapter 10 was about her hitting her pause button and journaling to uncover what was making her uneasy in her life. Martha's reflection was getting so cloudy with other parts of her life and journaling helped clear her way. However, when you decide to reflect, make it a priority to then incorporate the outcomes of your reflection into your Leadership Legacy.

Many times a leader will finally decide to do some deep reflection when forced into a situation. Below is an inspirational story from a leader who originally trained as a nurse, had her own business for the next 10 years, and then went back to college. Below is her forced reflection story.

PROFILE

What gives me inspiration? What a tough question to answer! Apart from showing my children how to be socially and financially responsible, I don't know. I can tell you the story of how I was inspired to go back to school:

I was in a hospital bed on bed rest after I had a tear in my amniotic sac at 19 weeks' gestation with my baby. I had a business at the time but the longer I lay in bed, the more I contemplated my future. I was tired of running all the financial aspects, proposal writings, client acquisition, and hiring of contractors. Especially with a newborn, I wanted a job I could leave at work. I had already run the business with two small children who were at the time in elementary school. The idea of doing it again with a newborn was very unappealing.

I felt as if I did not have a lot of choices. With my own business I had been out of the office setting for more than 10 years and was not too keen on returning to my original profession out of college, which had been nursing. An older nurse at the hospital had the following conversation with me.

NURSE: When did you graduate college?
ME: Sixteen years ago.
NURSE: And how long do you plan to work?
ME: Probably till I am 65 or so.
NURSE: How long is that?
ME: Twenty-seven years give or take.
NURSE: Then why do you feel you can't use a few of those years to go back to college and do something you really want to do?

> Seeing my future years in perspective of my younger self made me think differently. I had commiserated about choosing a degree my first time that was not a good match for me, but seeing it put in this manner made me rethink getting a different degree. I am now much happier with a science degree. Something my younger self would have never pursued but my older self was ecstatic to learn.
>
> I am very happy to be starting a serious career later in life. I just recently got a job in a field I find very interesting. I have also narrowed a gap between my children and myself. I understand their current issues, the social stresses, and what college life is like today. I can help them with difficult math homework and most important I have shown them it is never too late to change a path in life.

Sometimes the most distressing situations can give us clarity. I spent seven years working at Right Management, one of the top three global outplacement firms. During that time I worked with more than 2,000 people who had been let go by their employer. Almost all of them were let go not for their performance issues but because of needs of the business or restructuring. When these individuals first came to me, their emotions were raw, and their future was cloudy at best. I always honored those emotions and told them that there was life after this bump in their career road. To get them looking toward the future, they were taken through many of the exercises found in Part One of this book. They got to know themselves again and much of it was reflecting on their past successes (see Chapter 4) to begin to understand how much career currency they actually did have to spend. Just like the above story of reflecting on your life in a hospital bed, many found that the window had opened for them to make some changes and ultimately do more work that was in alignment with their strengths and personal values.

Being open to what life puts at your feet, taking the time to reflect, and being open to the inspiration that life brings our way is one of the best ways to unleash your Inner Leader.

It has been a long time, perhaps 15 years, since I met a director of customer contact in the power industry. We had some meetings, we discovered his strengths together, and to this day he lists his top five strengths in his e-mail signature. His passion for inspirational leadership was so strong that he embarked on a master's degree in coaching program with the University of North Carolina in Charlotte two years ago and is about to graduate. Much of his story is about authentically knowing yourself and celebrating yourself (see Part One). Below is his story of getting his inspiration from reflection.

PROFILE

I get my inspiration from many sources, all of which are derived from within. Most of my inspiration is innate and comes from my inner faith. I also get my inspiration from the wisdom of my foremothers and especially my grandmother who reared me. She was so encouraging and wise and I did not realize at the time that she was coaching and inspiring me. A saying from Grandma that inspires me is, *"You will never know if you can do something until you try it; at least once; as nothing beats a failure but a try."*

As we saw with previous inspirations, many believe that failure is the ultimate teacher, with the twist that says you must try anything that is important to you. Importance is the key for this person. While he continued his day job at the power company, he discovered the world of coaching and went back to school. For those who are searching for your Inner Leader, maybe it is just a matter of jumping in and trying it on!

My current HBA co-mentor, with whom I have worked for only a few months, sent me the following quote. If this is any indication of her level of leadership understanding, I am in for a great year of learning from her.

PROFILE

You have two choices: You can come down from the mountain and spend the rest of your days thinking it was so beautiful there, or you can create a vision, look upward, see the next mountain, and start the climb all over again.

—*Oprah Winfrey*

This quote reminds me of two very important elements of leadership. First, once a problem is solved, others will quickly fill its place on the list of issues, risks, and/or opportunities. As a leader, it is important to help the team stop for some reflection on that achievement. The conversation should not stop there but quickly turn to how that success gives us the experience and insights to tackle the next big one. Both a reflection on the road traveled and the vision of possibilities are important to leaders and teams.

This inspiration shows that reflection is important. Once you and your team have spent all this time climbing the mountain and coming down from it is the time to stop and hit the pause button to reflect: to reflect on the problem that you just solved, the project that was just completed, or the sale that was just made and celebrate the success that moved the team one step closer to being the experts that they want to be.

Her concept is not to just stop the conversation at the reflection point but to take the learnings of reflection into the future and do something with them. This could be shortened to *reflection is the way to vision*.

Have you been inspired by the stories in this section to reflect on the past to get to the future? What is your one big takeaway? What will you do in the future when you want to become inspired?

If you have been inspired and have a story to share, please send it to Coachvickie10@gmail.com and then you might be the one who will inspire others.

REFLECTING ON THE PAST TO GET TO THE FUTURE CHAPTER SUMMARY

- Stopping and hitting the pause button for reflection is essential for each of us to unleash our Inner Leader and ensure that we are going in the right direction.
- Reflection before projection ensures that we understand and celebrate past successes. Then the learnings of the reflection are incorporated into the projections of the future.
- Reflection can happen when a person is forced into a situation such as a job loss or a serious illness. That is when all the insights

learned in Part One of this book become increasingly important to use when projecting the future.

- Sometimes after reflection, fear of failure gets in the way of projection. Taking the view of failure being a road to success is a way of unleashing your Inner Leader.

- A successful leader reflects so that the conversation can then be directed to how that success gives the team the experience and insights to tackle the next big project.

CHAPTER 14

When *You* Become the Inspiration

When you unleash your Inner Leader you become the inspiration for others. This is your end goal, your dream, and your Leadership Legacy. The inspirational stories in this chapter are from people who simply spent their life doing their job, super well and to the best of their abilities. They then became inspirations to others. Finding out years later the inspiring effect that you had on people's lives is all about living your Leadership Legacy.

Asking others about the effect that you have had on their lives could be very inspiring to you. Living by your personal values is a key learning to a successful and enjoyable life.

As stated in the preface, I wrote this book to reach a broader audience so that more leaders, like you, could find your authentic selves and begin to build your Leadership Legacies.

WHEN *YOU* BECOME THE INSPIRATION

What happens when you unleash your Inner Leader and you live authentically? The answer is that you become the inspiration for others. This is your end goal, your dream, and your Leadership Legacy. There is no better gift that you can give to others than to be an inspirational leader who gives a legacy for others to enjoy and emulate.

The experiences shared with you below were great revelations in my request for inspirational stories. They were from people who simply spent their life doing their job super well and to the best of their abilities. Then guess what happened? At some point people whom they had influenced along the way took the time to come back to them and tell them how much they appreciated their influence. Then the real magic happened—instead of being humble and brushing off the compliments (see Chapter 5), they heartily embraced the praise and used it as a springboard to continue to build their Leadership Legacy. Let's read their stories; I promise that you will be inspired.

The first story is from my niece, with whom I interact at my husband's family reunion and in lots of fun times. We typically do not have serious conversations about what she has learned in life. I am honored to present her lesson, which is never to take anyone on this planet for granted and always to take the time to tell others what impact they have made on you. I knew that she was special, and I was so pleased that her Inner Leader had already been unleashed and that she was building her Leadership Legacy one student at a time.

PROFILE

My favorite quote is, "To the world you may be one person; to one person you may be the world."

As a former teacher of children with disabilities I often wondered where my efforts in their early years would lead them; did anything I do have an impact on their lives; did I help them grow as people? I didn't spend a lot of time reflecting on this until these three situations occurred.

One day I ran into a former student who was by this time a young adult who said to me his years (most students spent three years with me) in my classroom were his best school years ever. This was because not only did I hold him accountable for his behaviors and his own learning but also I sure knew how to have fun. I made school fun and something he looked forward to attending and he learned to look for the positives in every situation.

Next, I had a two-year position as a crisis counselor in a middle school with teens, mostly boys who had emotional and social disabilities as well as learning disabilities. These boys ran the streets more than track and were most definitely on the path to state-run facilities. One young man would run away from home, break into the school, and spend the night in my office. He told me he felt safer there than in his own home.

In another scenario, I became friends of the parents of a student after she left my program and have since remained an important part of their lives, celebrating many of life's moments with them. Most recently I celebrated her twenty-first birthday with them having a blast, of course and was told by her grandmother that to this day she cannot hear songs or see images of Elvis without thinking of me and the many years she was a part of the celebration of learning and loving life in my classroom.

Your impact on the people you encounter is never fully realized because we tend to take too many things for granted and one day we'll tell them or falsely believe they already know. Because of this saying and the three aforementioned incidents I try to no longer take the people in my life for granted, making sure I tell them how important they are to me often and why or what I have learned from them; I make it a ritual to be as kind as possible in every situation, being mindful that everyone is struggling with a different journey and a small act of kindness might make their day and to have a much fun as possible because life is too short!

This is a huge inspiration. Finding out years later the effect that you had on people's lives is all about living your Leadership Legacy. Here this woman was quietly going about her job and doing it the best way that she knows how. Then this wonderful unsolicited feedback came her way. Some people would have simply brushed it off and not done much with these rich words. Instead these words provided her the inspiration to go on and do more to help influence those around her.

These are not the stories that one wants to hear at the end of a project, a career, or a life; these are the stories that we want to hear as we are building and *living* our Leadership Legacy.

The following story of inspiration comes from a coaching session that I had with a medical doctor who has been leading a team of medical scientists in the pharmaceutical industry for the past decade.

We were developing his personal brand, and he told me his story, which follows:

PROFILE

When I was 12 years old my mother developed in incurable disease and I watched her slowly slip away from paralysis in a 20-year period. There was not a lot of information out there at that time and I decided to become a physician to help others not have this happen to them.

After my schooling I did my residency and beyond in some of the worst human immunodeficiency virus (HIV) clinics in the country. What I found was that these patients were mostly uneducated and had other social issues, all of which ... they turned to me for help and I gave it to them. After my wife died of cancer the clinic/patient world was just a little too much for me and I made a life change to industry, thinking that it would be a break for only a few years. In industry, I found so many smart and dedicated people who had career aspirations that I could help them with. It was exciting to me to build my entire team ... with clinical competence and with people who really cared about making a difference.

Together we began to craft this man's personal brand statement, talking about being a compassionate physician, a lifelong mentor, and a thought-driven leader. As our coaching time came to a close, I suggested to him that his short brand statement could be in the form of a question that he would use in every meeting, conference call, and conversation. It would be: What are we aspiring to in this (project, meeting, medical treatment, or presentation) that would make us be the best in the industry?

His answer, with a long exhale, was, "Wow, Vickie, that is really inspiring."

My response was, "Do you realize that you have been inspiring people all of your life from the young men with HIV who turned to you for more than medical treatment, to your decade in industry where past colleagues call you for career advice?"

He was amazed and ecstatic to have a mirror held up to him in a coaching session and to discover that his whole life he had been a lifelong mentor and inspiration to those around him, by simply being his authentic self and doing his job. (See Chapter 5 on personal branding.)

This man was truly an inspiration, and he did not fully grasp the effect that he had on people. The inspirational message is that many times we do not see the impact of our actions until someone who knows us well holds a mirror to our face and invites us to look inside. Once we realize the actions that we have consistently done over time, this then helps us understand the impact that we have made on others. I invite you to ask a trusted friend or colleague to do this for you. Invite this person to tell you what your impact on him or her has been. Ask this individual what it meant to him or her to have you in his or her life. Your impact might surprise you!

The following story came from someone whom I have never met. He has been reading my newsletters for years, presumably forwarded by a friend or colleague, and he subscribed later. When I called for input from my community, he responded with the following:

PROFILE

First, I want to thank you for your newsletters over the years. Although I am approaching my retirement years I still find your insights helpful.

My personal quotation that I have tried to live by has been:

Life isn't determined by moments spent breathing, but measured in increments of achieving.

For me, a day without learning something is a day wasted. Since I work in a high school my biggest motivator is being around students that are challenged by learning all day long. I look at this as a huge opportunity to dig into something that I never knew before and try to get students to look at each challenge as an opportunity to open a door.

My motivation is to get kids to see each of these challenges as a potential turning point in their lives. You never know when the smallest piece of information will become the key to solving a problem later in life.

When students tell me that they have learned more from me and my work than what they have learned in the classroom in four years I feel that I have totally fulfilled my mission.

By the way, I am the facility manager, not a teacher.

Oh my, I was left speechless, as I am sure that you are. Here is a person who has taken his Inner Leader to a very high level and was kind enough to share. His story is inspirational on so many levels. First, he lived by his personal values, and that learning was the key to a successful and enjoyable life. Second, he shared those values with the students and kept their world fun and interesting. And lastly, he was inspired by the feedback, reactions, and comments that he had gotten to share his story with us.

This is an example of a person who has unleashed his Inner Leader to the world.

I felt a fourth inspiration from this story. The story above gave *me* validation that as an executive business coach I have, in fact, been living *my* Leadership Legacy. By simply doing my job year over year, coaching clients, and sending out my monthly newsletter, I have inspired others to unleash their Inner Leader. I have never met this man and yet have inspired him to live in concert with his strengths, values, impact, and personal brand. This has always been my personal mission. Remember my statement from the beginning of this book: *My measure of success is the inspiration and success of the people whom I come in contact with.*

That is what I want to do, and the recognition is fulfilling and rewarding. It makes me determined to continue to impact the lives of others and help them live their Leadership Legacy.

As stated in the preface, I wrote this book to reach a broader audience so that more leaders, like you, could find your authentic selves and begin to build your Leadership Legacies. In other words, I want to *maximize* a global group of leaders' potential. If this book gives readers at least one *aha* moment, or if they deploy one new behavior that changes the way that they lead, or they achieve a success that they never thought possible, then my mission will be realized.

If you have been inspired and have a story to share, please send it to CoachVickie10@gmail.com and then you might be the one who will inspire others.

WHEN *YOU* BECOME THE INSPIRATION
CHAPTER SUMMARY

- When you unleash your Inner Leader you become the inspiration for others. This is your end goal, your dream, and your Leadership Legacy.

- The inspirational stories in this chapter are from people who simply spent their life doing their job super well and to the best of their abilities. They then became inspirations to others.

- Finding out years later the inspiring effect that you had on people's lives is all about living your Leadership Legacy.

- Asking others about the effect that you have had on their lives could be very inspiring to you.

- Living by your personal values is a key learning to a successful and enjoyable life.

- As stated in the preface, I wrote this book to reach a broader audience so that more leaders, like you, could find your authentic selves and begin to build your Leadership Legacies.

About the Author

Vickie Bevenour (Coach Vickie) is a Leadership Strategist. Using her natural passion for excellence, she inspires and activates business leaders to use their Inner Leader, all day, every day, to become the top 2 percent in *their* world. Her mission is to pave the path for leaders to truly embrace and leverage their Inner Leader into a series of achievements that translates into personal happiness, a purposeful legacy, and a world where living at the top of one's game is a constant state of being.

Clients and colleagues recognize Coach Vickie's keen ability to take things from good to great by inspiring and motivating others to identify the critical elements of their success, practice them regularly, and create them as habits. Across the board, her clients name "the connection of high achievement with personal happiness" as a key benefit of their coaching partnership with Vickie.

"A professional legacy is what one builds and lives every day ... Rather than a reminder of one's past, it is a proactive approach to the world on a daily basis." This quote from Vickie is threaded throughout her coaching approach and results in staggering achievements and legacies in her clients' lives. As an executive's partner and strategic muse, she shatters boundaries to creativity and challenges clients to stand outside of the box and consider all 360 degrees around them. In the past decade, she has proudly played a part in the success of more than 4,000 business leaders, in 17 countries, building their personal business legacies and helping them become business heroes.

Leading by example, Coach Vickie is constantly raising the bar for herself to cultivate her own Leadership Legacy through her private practice. *Ethical, energetic, worldly,* and *positive* are adjectives commonly associated with Vickie. From multimillion-dollar business leaders, to global executives, to organizations of several thousand, Vickie's methodology has been openly praised as "a vital and essential catalyst" to their legacy-grade success. Her no-nonsense approach is equally at home in the executive suite as well as working with evolving leaders pursuing education within prestigious business schools. Hand selected to provide coaching and customized programming to the master of business administration (MBA) programs within Duke University, Columbia University, and North Carolina State University, Vickie holds a special passion for instilling the foundations of professional legacy and happiness in each of these future leaders.

Vickie holds an MBA from Tulane University and a bachelor of arts from Randolph College and is a Professional Certified Coach (PCC) from the International Coach Federation. She is a Certified Personal Branding Strategist (CPBS), is a graduate of Coach University's Corporate Coaching Program, and has a Master's Certificate in Business Coaching from the University of North Carolina at Charlotte. She worked in the information technology industry for 23 years and has been the owner of her own coaching firm, The RDW Group, Inc., for the past 12 years.

Index